How to Survive the Recession and the Recovery

How to Survive the Recession and the Recovery

Anna Farago

with an introduction by Benj Gallander

INSOMNIAC PRESS

Edited by Mike O'Connor
Copy edited by Lorissa Sengara
Designed by Mike O'Connor

National Library of Canada Cataloguing in Publication Data

Farago, Anna, 1978-

How to survive the recession
Includes bibliographical references and index.

ISBN 1-894663-24-1

1. Finance, Personal. I. Title.

HG179.F363 2002   332.024   C2002-900771-2

The publisher gratefully acknowledges the support of the Canada Council, the Ontario Arts Council and the Department of Canadian Heritage through the Book Publishing Industry Development Program.

Printed and bound in Canada

Insomniac Press, 192 Spadina Avenue, Suite 403
Toronto, Ontario, Canada, M5T 2C2
www.insomniacpress.com

THE CANADA COUNCIL | LE CONSEIL DES ARTS
FOR THE ARTS | DU CANADA
SINCE 1957 | DEPUIS 1957

ONTARIO ARTS COUNCIL
CONSEIL DES ARTS DE L'ONTARIO

for Frances "Bunny" Zaza

I thank Mike O'Connor for the enormous opportunity he bestowed upon me. For some reason, he had steadfast faith in me and for that I am bewildered and grateful. I am also beholden to my copy editor Lorissa Sengara for her relentless pursuit of clarity.

To the Zazas, I am grateful for their benevolence and for accommodating me and my frenzied schedule throughout this project. I am indebted to Steve Stasiuk, for answering his phone and being a most insightful sounding board. I also thank my sister for allowing me to infiltrate her room and take her computer hostage, and Don Sedgwick for his advice and instruction.

For all other opportunities in my life, I thank my family. They have paved many roads for me, including this one, and the thanks they deserve cannot fit on a mere page.

Table of Contents

Chapter 2: Debt Management

Introduction

Benj Gallander, MBA

I am known as a contrarian investor. Many people think that those of my ilk are disagreeable, irascible, and quarrelsome. Let me assure you from the outset that this is not our purpose. Rather, there are times when it is quite obvious that standard thought is silly thought, based on anything but rationality. The truth is that contrarians carefully choose points in time to sit on the other side of the fence, and as investors, make their greatest returns by riding with the herd. A few years ago, I was being particularly ill tempered. As I'm sure you'll remember, the technology boom was in full swing and martinis and high living were the flavor of the day. The multitudes—many experts among them—hoisted their overflowing glasses to the demise of the business cycle and toasted never ending prosperity. And why not? The North American economy was enjoying its longest expansion ever. Wasn't it obvious that economic cycles just no longer applied? Long live growth and ever increasing productivity! The world had embraced a neoteric paradigm.

Being the skeptic that I amas well as a student of history, my conclusionwas that the celebratory bash for the death of enduring economic patterns was not only premature, but dare I say it, steeped in hokum. The business cycle was no more eliminated than death and taxes. Unfortunately, I have been proven correct with the latest recession that is now in full bloom. This is a pity, as I do love parties.

Why can continuous growth not occur? As Kenneth Boulding succinctly put it, "Anyone who believes exponential growth can go on forever in a finite world is either a madman or an economist."

Given that expansions and contractions will continue as long as humans inhabit this planet, the question becomes: how does one prepare for the downturns? Certainly the glory days of expansion require less consideration as one basks in the good times. Ignoring the need for preparation for when the bubble bursts, however, is folly. The fact is that the preparation work for recessionary, and even depressionary times, takes place when the going is good. Remember the old parable: during the fat years, one should prepare for the lean. And during the lean, one must practice cautionary measures.

This is not meant to suggest for a moment that boom times should not be relished. Instead my advice is to be realistic about the fact that as certainly as winter follows fall, a recession is rarely far away and expedience will serve you well. By planning ahead, coping with the difficult times will be easier. That is what this book is all about: a primer to both plan for the future, and also to live as well as possible with the difficulties that a recession brings.

How to Survive the Recession and the Recovery offers a gamut of information. It commences with a historical perspective on past recessions that is exceedingly worthwhile for understanding how to survive future downturns. Later, the book outlines the basics of preparing and dealing with a slump, while also providing in-depth solutions to real situations. The book outlines a methodology to deal with an economic cycle over which you have no control, by practicing a personal business cycle via a budget that will aid you to withstand the arduous times. By following the outline in this book, your highs might initially be a little lower, but your lows will certainly not be as low. Overall, by maintaining a modicum of prudence, both your lows and highs can be more elevated, as your preparation for both the short- and long-terms will create benefits hitherto unimagined.

One of the beauties of *How to Survive the Recession and the Recovery* is that it is not only useful at a particular point in time, but over a long duration. Any of us who live to a ripe age will experience numerous declines during our lifetimes. While we like to believe every downturn is unique, for the most part, contending with each downturn requires virtually the same fundamental readiness and skills.

Place this book in a prominent place among the books in your home. Eevery so often, remember to plan for your future and that of your loved ones. Knowledge helps create security, and there is no time when protection is more valuable than when times are arduous and uncertain.

Benj Gallander writes a column, "The Contra Guys," each month in the Globe and Mail. *He is the author of* The Uncommon Investor *(Insomniac, 1998).*

Chapter 1
History and Anatomy

Part I: History of Recessions

Understanding past recessions is crucial to surviving future recessions. Since the Great Depression ended in 1940, both Canada and the United States have recovered from each recession they have faced; this has been due, in part, to the fact that more and more people recognize that the economy has its peaks and valleys, and that recessions call for strategy, not distress.

The Great Depression and the New Deal

Over the last century, the federal government has progressively become more involved in the economy, through bank security, exchange regulations, banking regulations, progressive taxation systems, and targeted government spending. In reality, we as individuals have

Breadline in Chicago during the Depression

very little control over the value of our dollar—we can count our money all we want, but we cannot control what it counts for.

Before the New Deal was instituted in the United States in the 1930s, money represented something tangible—gold. Every dollar floating around the market represented a piece of gold that was sitting in a bank vault somewhere. In theory, anyone who had some money could walk into a bank and cash in their dollars for gold. If the international worth of gold fell, a country would have to scramble to find more gold in the hypothetical event that its dollars were cashed in. This was known as the gold standard: the economy of a particular country controlled by the worth of gold around the globe. The gold standard did not function perfectly, though. Because of rapid inflation and a corresponding devaluation of currency during the 1920s, the U.S. possessed only enough gold to reimburse one twenty-fifth of the American population for their dollars at the time of the Great Depression in 1929. However, the New Deal effectively dismantled the gold standard, and today money is no longer representative of an object like gold; money is simply numbers.

The New Deal is credited with bringing about the drastic changes that the North American economy underwent after the Great Depression. In the early

1930s, the aftermath of the First World War and the advent of the Great Depression, meant that U.S. President Herbert Hoover was faced with a great many economic decisions, including the question of the controversial Bonus Bill, which had been passed in 1924. In 1931, Texas congressman Wright Patman began issuing payments in accordance with the bill that awarded veterans $1 for each day that they had spent in the war, and $1.25 per day for veterans who had spent time overseas. Hoover was opposed to these payments, arguing that the plan would cost the Treasury $4 billion, so he cut payments. The veterans' reaction was fierce and visible; many were left with no savings, no homes, and no jobs. The battle between the veterans and the government persisted until Hoover lost the 1932 presidential election by a landslide to Franklin D. Roosevelt. By this time, the economic depression had deepened.

The New Deal was President Roosevelt's emergency response to the injured economy. New Deal legislation created employment for a quarter of a million unemployed Americans, and implemented a break on taxes and standards for minimum wages, working hours, and security. Other policies re-authorized the sale of beer, which was outlawed durng the 1920s under Prohibition, creating added employment and revenue. Banking, agriculture, social security and public welfare were put under federal authority. The New Deal also set the gears in motion for the future expansion of labor unions in the steel, automobile and rubber indus-

Franklin D. Roosevelt

tries. The farm and industrial recov-

Women entered the work force in unprecedented numbers during the Second World War

ery acts helped control speculative excess, which will be discussed in further detail later in this chapter, and also raised employment rates.

The New Deal was not wholly responsible for the return of a stable economy in North America at the end of the 1930s, however: the Second World War revived American industry and effectively ended the Great Depression. With American men going off to fight in the war in vast numbers, jobs opened up everywhere. Productivity shot up in leaps and bounds to meet the great demand for resources for the war effort. Abandoned factories were reopened, failing businesses were refashioned to supply goods needed for the war and workers were rehired, with many women were being hired for the first time. Roosevelt also passed the Servicemen's Readjustment Act of 1944, otherwise known as the GI Bill, which was a revised and expanded version of the Bonus Bill. The GI Bill gave veterans unemployment pay, education and housing with no money down.

1945–1950

After the Second World War ended, the economy entered an economic bubble. The rate at which productivity, the employment rate and the population were growing indicated that economic expansion was progressing at a dangerous rate. Many Americans feared that the economy would flounder again after the productivity generated by the war ceased and soldiers returned home to rejoin the labor force. However, the post-war period was marked by consumer demand following the demobilization of more than 15 million American servicemen. The housing sector experienced a boom: houses were very affordable under the provisions of the GI Bill, and the increase in the birth rate after the war created a demand for dwellings for millions of new families. Between 1920 and 1950, the American population increased by 30%, but the country's total number of dwellings increased by 51%. Industries that had grown while producing military goods now produced consumer goods more efficiently. The GNP rose from about US$100 million in 1940 to US$200 million in 1950.

Prior to the Second World War Canada was primarily known for agriculture and natural resources. After the war ended, however, Canada was the world's third-largest industrial producer. The Canadian government erected trade barriers around the country, tightening control over how much competition would be allowed in and the Canadian economy experienced the same fast paced expansion as the United States.

Unfortunately, the economy could not handle such a dramatic expansion after such a severe depression. The housing boom encouraged by the GI Bill became a new problem. With no money down required, families were buying houses more quickly than builders could build them. Toward the end of the 1940s, the pace of ecomomic expansion became too fast and the bubble burst. The Great Depression loomed large in many people's minds, and with a recession materializing, many feared that the country would slip back into a depression. People began to panic. So why did the recession of 1949 not turn into a depression like its predecessor? For one thing, because the New Deal had forever changed the value of money, the panic to run to the bank was not as great. In an effort to limit inflation in light of rising national income and scarce consumer products, the newly created Office of Price Administration controlled rents on some dwellings, rationed consumer items ranging from sugar to gasoline and otherwise tried to restrain price increases. The value of money was more abstract and less corporeal, so more investors stayed put. The recession equalized the economy in 1950, after two roller-coaster decades of depression and war.

1950–1960

At mid-century, the landscape of America was changing due to the affordability of cars. People in general were wealthier and cars were cheap, which created an opportunity for residential development to spread beyond city limits. By 1940, 13 million people lived in communities beyond the reach of public transportation, and by the 1950s suburban life had carved a spot in society. Within the economy, the service industry grew to surpass the trade industry. Because of automatization of industrial production, there were eventually more people providing services than producing goods. As a result of a slight saturation in both the service and trade sectors, the economy experienced a brief recession in 1953 and 1954.

Under the supervision of President Dwight D. Eisenhower, inaugurated in 1953, the Department of Health, Education and Welfare was created. Rights to health care and other benefits were extended to the less fortunate within society, which created a broader spectrum of consumers. White-collar and blue-collar jobs both underwent change. White-collar jobs, which were previously reserved for the wealthy, were opened up to the middle class laborer, and by 1956, more Americans occupied white-collar jobs than blue-collar ones. Blue-collar work changed as the labor unions began to win their ongoing battles for long-term employment contracts and other benefits for their members. The rich and the poor were bridging a gap in the labor force.

Dwight D. Eisenhower

On the other hand, the agricultural sector went through tough times as productivity exceeded demand. Farming was being taken over by large companies that bought up large amounts of land and could subsequently produce consumable goods more efficiently than the smaller, family-owned farms were able to. Many farmers left their land and were consequently unemployed; meanwhile large corporate farms mass-produced and saturated the market. The quick expansion of the farm industry and a resulting saturation of the produce market caused another brief recession in 1957.

However, in general, the latter part of the 1950s was all about growth. The federal government supported the construction of highways, which fostered the growth of residential areas away from the city core. Land was rapidly developed for housing. Malls were a fairly new addition to American culture in the 1950s and quickly popped up all over the country. The overdevelopment of land that attended suburban growth actually caused the economy to fall into another brief recession in 1960 and 1961.

1960–1970

President Eisenhower left the White House in January 1961, and a young newcomer stepped up to the plate. John F. Kennedy was elected president in 1960 as the face of North America was on the brink of a dramatic change. The 1950s in America are often spoken of as a time of complacency; the 1960s, however, brought many new issues such as the environment, race relations, poverty and quality of life to the forefront of national debate. Kennedy's administration responded to these concerns by establishing programs and policies to deal with social problems. Kennedy created the Peace Corps, which employed young Americans and offered material and financial assistance to developing countries overseas. After Kennedy's assassination in 1963, his successor Lyndon B. Johnson continued this work, creating programs to help conserve the environment and provide medical assistance for the poor and the elderly. At the same time, federal spending was poured into the space program and the Vietnam War. The initiatives of Kennedy and Johnson allowed the decade to progress smoothly, economically speaking, with only one small recession in 1966.

1970–1980

In 1973 and 1974, the U.S. experienced a benchmark recession that lasted sixteen months. The problem dated back to 1943 when Venezuela had signed the first "fifty-fifty principle" agreement, which gave oil producers a

Oil drilling rig in Alberta.

fifty-fifty split of the profits in their contracts with importers. Arab producers quickly followed suit and insisted upon similar agreements with oil buyers. After the Second World War ended, the demand for oil began to rise rapidly. The abundance of oil supply should have saturated the market and caused the price of oil to drop, but it didn't. The problem was that oil-producing countries were still being paid a fixed price for oil. Foreign oil producers were making high profits and could invest more money into their oil production, causing the market price to fall even further, while still being paid a fixed price for their oil. Domestic producers like Texas, Oklahoma, and Louisiana could not compete. Eisenhower feared that the U.S.'s dependence on foreign oil suppliers could jeopardize the domestic economy and imposed an import quota on oil, which brought domestic oil prices down to compete with the world price. Prices spiraled lower and lower as foreign oil producers began to cut their posted prices down in order to regain lost profits.

The Organization of Petroleum Exporting Countries (OPEC) was formed by Iran, Iraq, Kuwait, Saudi Arabia, and Venezuela in 1960 with the purpose of putting a halt to free-falling oil prices. The founding members were later joined by Qatar (1961), Indonesia (1962), Libya (1962), the United Arab Emirates (1967), Algeria (1969), Nigeria (1971), Ecuador (1973), and Gabon (1975). By 1970, OPEC's share of world oil production had risen from 28% in 1960 to 41%. In 1972, the price of crude oil was a stable three dollars per barrel; however, the rising demand for oil began to exceed production. OPEC was in a position of power over the U.S. producers because the United States did not have enough crude oil to serve its own demand and OPEC controlled a large portion of the foreign supply.

In October 1973, war broke out between Egypt and Israel. Saudi Arabia refused to increase its oil production in order to bring prices down in the United States unless the U.S. backed the Arab position. When President Richard Nixon publicly expressed support for Israel, the Arab states began an oil embargo against the U.S. Crude oil prices rose to twelve dollars a barrel. The U.S., along with the rest of the world, entered a deep recession.

President Gerald Ford tookpower in August 1974. His response to the recession was to impose price controls on domestically produced oil to make consumption of domestic oil more appealing than imported oil. (With these controls in place, imported oil was 48% more expensive than domestic.) Ford also administered a tax cut for low- to moderate-income families in order to stimulate consumption. He put a stop to excessive federal expenditures and cut back on funding for many existing federal programs. Small businesses were granted a tax break to encourage expansion and create more jobs. The country eventually recovered from the recession, but extremely slow growth and a general economic malaise characterized the second half of the 1970s.

1980–1990

In 1980, Ronald Reagan was elected president on a platform of reducing both taxes and the size of the federal government. When he entered office, the economy was teetering on the brink of a recession. As an answer, Reagan's administration championed supply-side economics.

Before the recession of the 1970s, inflation and unemployment rates were correlated: if inflation was high, unemployment was low; and if inflation was low, unemployment rates tended to be high. Officials usually attempted to engineer lower unemployment by increasing the national money supply through the Federal Reserve, which encouraged an increase in inflation. In the 1970s,

Ronald Reagan

this correlation started to unravel. Businesses began to raise prices in *anticipation* of higher inflation, and people started losing their jobs because production and consumer spending fell. The result was an increase in inflation *and* unemployment.

The central concept of Reagan's supply-side economics was that tax cuts would cause economic growth. Entrepreneurs would invest their tax savings, creating higher productivity as well as more jobs and profits.

With a lower tax rate applied to higher profits and wages, entrepreneurs and workers would end up paying more taxes in total than before the cuts. Theoretically, the government could generate spending and productivity, which would lower unemployment and maintain a manageable rate of inflation without having to increase the money supply. Supply-side theory was not far from trickle-down economics. Trickle down economics purports that giving tax cuts to the wealthy will eventually "trickle down" the gains to benefit the middle class. In theory, these tax cuts would benefit businesses in the form of profit, which would, in turn, allow the businesses to increase employee wages or benefit packages. The idea is that better-payed employees would stimulate the economy, and in turn, create more jobs. The theory was difficult to digest if you were not in a high income bracket because the profits from tax breaks were not always turned around in the form of increased pay. Reagan may not have been so highly revered in the 1980 election had trickle-down been an explicit part of his platform.

Unfortunately, supply-side economics were only good on paper. The national debt continued to mount for seven out of the eight years Reagan was in office. Unemployment did go down due to Reagan's reduction in marginal taxes, which made it more profitable to work increased hours and maintain dual-income families, but that did not create the consumer market the administration had hoped for. The economy entered recession in 1981. The recession of 1981–1982 lasted a longer-than-average sixteen months, with a negative growth of 2.2%, the highest percent of negative growth since the Second World War.

In Canada, exaggerated expectations in commodity prices prior to 1981 had led to excessive investment in the Canadian resource sector. The nation was immersed in a deep recession throughout 1982. Every sector of the economy was affected, from the service industry to agriculture. The rate of business bankruptcies rose 50%.

North America's recovery from this lengthy recession was the result of a drop in oil prices, a very strict distribution of money and credit from the Federal Reserve in the U.S. and the Bank of Canada, and governmental regulation of food prices to help the agricultural sectors recovery.

Following the recovery, the American economy entered into a long expansion that lasted until the end of the decade. Inflation and unemployment remained low and steady growth led to higher standards of living. The annual inflation rate remained under 5% from 1983 through 1987. Many referred to this state as the "Goldilocks" economy because economic activity was not high enough to cause high inflation and not low enough to cause unemployment—it was just right.

1990–present

The economy stabilized following the devastating recession of the early 1980s, but by the end of Reagan's presidency the national debt had increased by $2 trillion. Droughts in the late 1980s adversely affected the farming sector. Slow growth and a stock-market crash in the late 1980s had left the financial sector on shaky ground. The turmoil continued into the early 1990s with savings-and-loan companies. Scandals resulted when savings-and-loan companies grossly overvalued their assets, especially in real estate. The federal government had to come to the rescue in many cases, which increased debts even further.

A new recession began in 1990, a month before the U.S. and its allies entered the Gulf War. The war exacerbated the slump, causing the recession to last until March 1991.

Following another slump in 1993, North America experienced almost eight years of steady economic growth. In 1994, the North American Free Trade Agreement (NAFTA) was signed as the economy began to recover. NAFTA is an agreement between Canada, the U.S. and Mexico, which has created the world's largest free-trade area by allowing almost all trade between Canada and the U.S. to be conducted tariff-free. (The benefits and dangers of NAFTA have been widely debated, but the agreement did precede one of the longest periods of consistent economic growth.)

The electronic age flourished as a result of the introduction of the World Wide Web in 1992. By 1998, 100 million people were online. The national debt was down, quality of life was up, and growth was expanding at a healthy rate. The National Bureau of Economic Research (NBER) has stated that the prolonged expansion ended in March 2001.

In the early years of a new century, the information technology engine that helped fuel the last and longest period of economic expansion is on shaky ground. The expectations and projections for the IT companies were unrealistic. As a result, many are out of business; those that survive have severely reduced their operations.

Recessions over the past century have become shorter, and in turn, the expansion periods between economic downturns have become longer. Federal Reserve Chairman Alan Greenspan believes that "the American economy has become increasingly resilient to shocks." North Americans today are responsive to low interest rates, tax cuts and new spending. The word "recession" does not breed panic as it did in the era of the Great Depression. In the past, the terrorist attacks of September 11 might have been a fatal wound to the economy, but with today's controlled, educated responses to economic ups and downs, recessions are a natural regulating element in the economy.

Part II: Anatomy of a Recession

What is a Recession?

The technical definition of a recession is two or more consecutive quarters of a year in which the Gross National Product (in the U.S.) and Gross Domestic Product (in Canada) show a decline or negative growth. The Gross Domestic Product, or GDP, is calculated by determining the total market value of the Gross National Product, or GNP, plus the income earned by domestic residents through foreign investments and minus the income earned in domestic markets by foreign citizens. The difference between the GNP and the GDP is that the GDP represents the value of all production within national borders, regardless of whether the labor and property value accounted for in the total is domestic- or foreign-owned, while the GNP considers the foreign market in its equation.

GDP = Goods + Services + Products

GNP = GDP + Income earned by domestic residents from foreign investments - Income earned by foreigners in the domestic market

The National Bureau of Economic Research, which was established in 1920 and is now the nation's leading non-profit economic research organization, defines the term "recession" slightly differently: "a recession begins just after the economy reaches a peak of activity and ends as the economy reaches its trough." The National Bureau of Economic Research's reasoning is that GNP/GDP statistics are not sufficiently accurate because some economic activity is anomalous and does not fit the "two quarters of negative growth" definition. The 1960 recession did not encompass two consecutive quarters of decline and the 1980 recession consisted of only one quarter of straight decline. The economy is never completely stagnant; expansion is its normal state. Therefore, a recession occurs after a high point in the level of economic activity and results in a drop in the GNP (or GDP) over two or more quarters, which is then followed by a recovery and a return to a normal state of economic expansion.

What should be evident so far is that the economy tends to run in a cycle. Recessions are not necessarily the result of poor economic management, although poor decisions can prolong or increase the severity of a recession. In fact, recessions are a component in the natural elasticity of the economy; if the economy expands at an unhealthy rate, a recession will keep the economy in check.

At this point you might be wondering: what determines an economic cycle? Good question, but difficult to answer. In the nineteenth century, the prevailing belief was that the economy was supposed to run smoothly and consistently; even minor fluctuations were regarded as crises. This century, however, business cycles are regarded as an innate and characteristc feature of economic life. What is not unanimously agreed upon, however, is what cycles are. A number of competing theories attempt to explain their existence.

The Kondratieff Cycle

The Kondratieff cycle is the longest proposed cycle, theorized as lasting an average of fifty-four years. Nikolai Dmytriyevich Kondratieff (1892–1930) worked at the Agricultural Academy and Business Research Institute in Moscow. His research focuses on the major economies of the early twentieth century, specifically those of the U.S., Great Britain, Germany and France. His cycle concentrates on what he called the "long wave."

According to Kondratieff, the long wave is more than half a century long and has four stages—boom, recession, depression and recovery.

He believed the wave to be an inherent part of the capitalist economy. His studies focused on wholesale prices and how they fit into his lengthy cycle, analyzing the production and consumption of major resources at the time and adjusting his figures to allow for changes in the population. His studies did not receive much attention in his lifetime or after his death until others began noticing lengthy economic cycles. An influencial supporter of the Kondratieff cycle was W. H. Beveridge (1879–1963). Lord Beveridge studied wheat prices and identified cycles occurring every fifty to sixty years dating back to the 1500s. The U.S. experienced two lengthy waves in the early 1900s that supported Kondratieff's cycle. Further studies have found that the "Kondratieff wave" tends to be set off by major technological advances, such as the automobile or the railroad.

The Kuznets Cycle

Simon Kuznets (1901–1985), an American economist who carried out research on the U.S. real-estate market, proposed another lengthy cycle theory. According to Kuznets, economic cycles last about twenty years. His research focused on population changes from generation to generation and took careful note of increases and decreases in the construction of housing. His theory was more popular when migration and immigration were occurring at high rates in the United States, but has since decreased in currency. There is, however, merit to his cycle theory, because many of the peaks and troughs in the economy do appear to bear relation to demographic changes—and his cycle is one of the few that takes into account such demographics.

The Juglar Cycle

Another theory of business cycles consists of waves of seven to eleven years in length. This cycle is named after Clement Juglar (1819–1905), a French economist who studied the rise and fall of interest rates and prices in the 1860s. Juglar knew that the business cycle and the credit cycle were related, he just didn't know why. His research spurred many of the overinvestment theories that are the basis of much economic discussion today.

His cycle is an industrial cycle: it is related to rates of investment in industrial equipment and plants. Juglar identified four phases to each economic wave: prosperity, crisis, liquidation and recession.

Successors to Juglar's research went on to develop the cycle more thoroughly. Mikhail I. Tugan Baranovsky claimed that the peak of the Juglar cycle, which is the beginning of a recession, occurs when financing runs out, but capital-producing industries are still running; subsequently, investment dwindles and these industries falter. After this period, loanable funds are built up in banks again, and these funds are then transformed into fixed capital, such as machinery. The economy gets ready for another expansion, which begins once the banking sector is ready to start lending again.

The Kitchin Cycle

Joseph Kitchin theorized a different business cycle based on the rhythm of fluctuation in business inventories. The cycle is derived from an article that Kitchin published entitled "Review of Economic Statistics." He had conducted a study of statistics relating to the American and British economies from 1890 to 1922 and found that price movements could be forecasted over a thirty-nine-month period, from recession to recession.

According to the Kitchin cycle, the progression is as follows. Interest rates peak and the money supply increases, but the public's demand for credit declines. In response, short-term interest rates are lowered. As a result, stocks decrease in value and investors start to anticipate better times ahead. As recovery is established, commodity prices decline. Economic activity accelerates, causing interest rates to very gradually increase and demand for credit to build. Eventually, interest rates become high enough to compete with anticipated earnings on the stock markets. Business activity booms and commodity prices increase because of demand. High interest rates, coupled with a contraction in the money supply from the central bank, push commodity prices down and the next recession begins.

Multiplier Effect

One of the most influential voices in the economic world this century has been John Maynard Keynes (1901–1964). Keynes was the first to propose the radical idea of spending money we don't have—the widely known income-expenditure multiplier effect. The basic idea was simple. People need to stay employed, especially when the economy slows down. In slow times, Keynes proposed, governments should run a deficit in order to keep people working, because the private sector does not invest enough when the economy is slow and people aren't spending. Lower investment leads to fewer jobs and less consumption. With the government picking up the slack, the economy may not be balanced, but people are still working and spending, which encourages renewed investing. Hyman P. Minsky (1919–1997) expanded on Keynes' theory, arguing that economic booms are prompted most crucially by an expansion in bank credit.

The idea of economic cycles is not accepted by everyone. Some believe cycles fail to account for outside forces that could rock the economy. Others believe the economy, in the long term, is unaffected by occurrences outside the macroeconomic system, so there is no need to consider things like the start and end of wars, or droughts. Economic cycles are difficult to understand and to detect because, while the theories may be supported by historical information, there is always a degree of speculation involved in applying them to current circumstances.

The anatomy of the economy is as important as the anatomy of a recession. Again, there are a number of formulas out there for recessions, but they are not as diverse as economic cycle theory.

The Four Bs

Bubble

A recession begins with a bubble. Speculative excess in the economy causes certain economic sectors to expand at an unhealthy rate, from overtrading, overspending or overproducing. In recessions of the past twenty years, speculative excess has involved buying commodities for resale rather than for use, or buying financial assets for resale rather than for income. A good example is the real-estate bubble that occurred in the early 1990s. Land was cheap, and many people bought real estate in the hopes of making profits through reselling their properties quickly. The problem was that since so many had invested in real estate with the same hope of resale profit, there were few buyers. The information-technology industry was dealt a similar hand in the late 1990s. The expansion of the IT industry happened so quickly and dramatically that companies' resources soon dramatically surpassed the demand for IT services. Unrealistic expectations in the economy, coupled with speculative excess, create bubbles that grow large and eventually burst.

Buzz

Be wary of a buzz in the market. Essentially buzz is what people are talking about in the market—from what sectors and stocks are hot, to speculation on the general state of the economy. How people react to the buzz can lead to various changes in the economy. For example, when a buzz has been created around a certain sector or product, insiders start to evaluate and re-evaluate their stocks, their assets and other investments. Sometimes when a buzz has been created around an unstable or declining economy, people begin to pull their money out of the market, or the government begins reviewing policies, or the Federal Reserve tightens interest rates—reactions vary. In this way, the reaction to a declining economy can determine how a recession will run its course—this is why it is important to keep in mind how the economy can be "talked" into a recession during the buzz stage. For example, at the start of the Great Depression, the public reaction to the economic downturn caused a great panic, which in turn forced the market into an even greater decline.

Another example of the potential dangers of buzz is the recession of 1961, which began shortly after problems arose in the steel industry. Steel companies butted heads with their workers over the issue of raising the price of steel. The companies eventually reneged on the bargain they had made with workers and raised prices. The media covered the conflict, and all related stocks plummeted quickly even though the conflict affected an isolated area of the market.

When the economy dips, however, a buzz can happen

without a real threat of a recession. If there is fear of an oncoming recession, the repercussions of a buzz can sometimes occur before the recession is officially, statistically determined. Take, for example, the market crash of 1987. The stock market declined in 1987, but had little overall effect on the economy. Had the media focused on the buzz around the declining economy, the public could have panicked and consumer confidence might have decreased sharply. Ultimately, the economic growth dropped slightly that quarter but a recession was avoided.

Burst

The bubble eventually bursts and the burst is the recession. Keep in mind that speculative excess in single sectors of the market rarely brings about recession. Many variables are involved, but average consumers should take note of bubbles that involve consumer spending, such as real estate, or information-technology investing, as changes in these sectors are most likely to affect large groups. Indicators differ from recession to recession, but in general, during a burst, productivity goes down, unemployment goes up.

Bandage

The bandage stage follows the burst. While not all economists believe that the economy is controllable, in most cases of a recession, a number of remedies are applied to stabilize the economy. The government refashions policies, enacts bank holidays, applies tax cuts or uses one of many other possible modification techniques. Often the bandage comes from the Federal Reserve Bank or changes to monetary policy to repair the economy.

Federal Reserve Bank

Between 1863 and 1914, the United States experienced a series of banking panics—in 1863, 1873, 1884, 1890, 1893 and 1907. It was the last panic—occurring in a time of general prosperity—that led to the creation of the Federal Reserve, established through the Federal Reserve Act, approved by President Wilson on December 23, 1913. The act allowed for the establishment of up to twelve Federal Reserve district banks to coordinate policy with the Federal Reserve Board.

The Federal Reserve system was designed to serve as a stabilizing force that would be a lender of last resort in times of crisis. At the same time it would oversee the provision of a national currency that would expand and contract as needed in an effort to prevent financial panic and economic depression.

Today, the Federal Reserve System—more commonly referred to as simply "the Fed"—consists of twelve Federal Reserve Banks strategically located in various major American cities. Along with a Federal Reserve Board of Governors, they are responsible for the system's long-term vision and its short-term actions.

The Fed plays a key role in North America's economic progress. Some might disagree, arguing that it wasn't able to prevent the Great Depression. Others, however, believe the Fed is largely responsible for the fact that we have never experienced an economic disaster of comparable magnitude since. The Fed is usually credited with stemming the negative effects of the October 1987 stock-market plunge.

While its initial mandate was to remain a passive institution, the Fed now plays a very active role in determining and maintaining the direction of our economy. In addition to its primary objective of promoting economic stability through effective monetary policy, the Fed is also a bank for banks, a bank for the U.S. government and a regulator of many of the United States' financial institutions—including all nationally chartered banks.

Monetary Policy

Monetary policy is the way in which the Federal Reserve helps guide the performance of the U.S. economy on a short-term basis by influencing the availability and cost of money and credit. The goals of an effective monetary policy are maximum employment, stable prices and moderate long-term interest rates. Monetary policy also tries to prevent excessive inflation, which can result when the supply of money grows too quickly in relation to the ability of businesses to produce goods and services. On the other hand, if the supply of money grows too slowly, the potential for unemployment and recession increases. When consumers have less money to spend, businesses are forced to reduce the prices of their goods and services, which means they have less to spend on resources—including labor. The Fed's constant challenge is to try to avoid both of these extremes.

So how does monetary policy affect the availability of money and credit? There are basically four ways:

The Fed can *put* more money in the economy by *buying* government securities on the open market. The money a seller receives gets deposited into a financial institution, which then sets aside a legislated percentage of the money on reserve and loans out the remainder. The borrower of this money now buys goods and services and the money from these business transactions gets deposited in various financial institutions, which again set aside a portion on reserve and loan out the rest. This process goes on and on, all the while increasing the amount of money circulating in the economy.

The Fed can *take* money out of the economy by *selling* government securities. In this case, money comes out of bank accounts in order to purchase the securities, which means that financial institutions then have less money to lend. This policy is used to gradually bring inflationary tendencies under control.

On rare occasions, the Fed will opt to raise or lower the reserve requirements of financial institutions. Lowering the percentage means banks have more money available for lending, while raising the percentage means that less money is available.

Even more rare is the decision to raise or lower the interest rate that financial institutions are charged when they borrow money from the Fed.

For all the good that monetary policy does and is capable of doing, its effectiveness is almost entirely dependent upon the foresight of those who set its course. Is it a reliable indicator of economic direction? Not likely. It is more often a reaction to economic direction—a variety of short-term adjustments that are necessary in order to stay on the track to a long-term goal. Fortunately, experience, technology and global influence are having positive effects on our ability to both predict and prevent dramatic economic downturns.

Indicators

In reality, the economy is difficult to predict and the composition of a recession can vary. There are some main economic indicators that provide an idea of how the economy will perform in the near future.

Employment

A general economic guideline is that if the unemployment rate is increasing, the economy is headed into a recession. When unemployment rises, the economy is not producing enough to maintain and create jobs. Correlatively, consumers have less money to purchase goods and services. Employment usually decreases because output, another economic indicator, is decreasing.

Output

The GDP, which represents the value of the total quantity of goods and services produced in the U.S. (or Canadian) economy in one year, measures a particular economy's output. The GDP is presented in two ways: in current dollars, which shows the market value of all goods and services produced, and in constant dollars. The second calculation factors in inflation and is known as real GDP. Real GDP is used to define the rate of economic growth. The GDP is provided quarterly by the Bureau of Economic Analysis of the U.S. Department of Commerce. The figures are available during the third or fourth week of every month.

Industrial Production Index

The industrial production index (IPI) gauges the output of the manufacturing, mining and utilities industries—in effect measuring the total quantity of physical means the physical items produced within the economy. If the IPI is low, the economy is not in good shape. The Federal Reserve Board prepares the IPI monthly. The figures are available in the middle of the month following the month to which they refer.

Capacity Utilization Rate

Capacity Utilization Rate (CUR) is a calculation related to the same industries covered by the industrial production index: manufacturing, mining and utilities. The CUR measures the proportion of industrial infrastructure capacity (plants and equipment) currently being used in production. When production rises quickly, the CUR increases, and when production slows or declines, the CUR decreases. The capacity index is used to help determine the greatest level of output a plant can maintain within the framework of a realistic work schedule. Capacity utilization over 85% usually generates inflation. The Federal Reserve Board presents the CUR monthly. It is available in the middle of the month following the month to which it refers, one day after the industrial production index.

Interest Rates

In the period prior to a recession, interest rates are raised in an attempt to slow the economy when it is perceived to be growing too quickly. To achieve this, the Federal Reserve Bank buys government securities, which reduces banks' reserve accounts, making banks more cautious about handing out loans. The accompanying higher interest rates tend to slow the economy.

The Federal Reserve Bank can also reverse this process to stimulate the economy. Government securities are bought back, increasing banks' reserves, driving interest rates lower and contributing to economic expansion.

Exchange Rates and PPP

The currency-exchange rate effectively measures one

country's economy against another's. The value of the dollar is relevant in the economy because it affects the prices charged for domestically-produced goods sold abroad as well as the cost of foreign goods bought domestically. Exchange rates do not always accurately measure real price differences between countries, however. The most accurate measurement involves purchasing price parity (PPP) rates. While exchange rates are based on the international market prices of currencies, PPPs are rates that show the real purchasing power of currencies. An easy way to determine the PPP values of certain currencies is to consult the "Big Mac Index," calculated regularly by *The Economist*. The Big Mac Index is a comparison of the price of a McDonald's Big Mac hamburger in various countries. For example, in April 2000, the price of a Big Mac was US$2.51 in the United States and CDN$2.85 in Canada. The PPP value of the Canadian dollar is $2.51 divided by $2.85, or $0.88, meaning that the Canadian dollar carries 88% of the purchasing power of one American dollar. The Canadian dollar was trading at US$0.68 at the time. The fact that its PPP value was $0.20 more than the open-market exchange rate, however, suggests that the Canadian dollar was worth $0.20 more in real terms than the exchange rate would indicate.

Producer Price Index

The Producer Price Index (PPI) measures prices at the wholesale level only, tracking the rate of price changes among domestically-produced goods in the manufacturing, mining, agriculture, and utility industries. While it does not measure actual inflation, the PPI is viewed as a leading indicator of inflation. The Bureau of Labor Statistics in the U.S. Department of Labor provides the PPI monthly. The figures are published in middle of the month immediately following the month to which they refer.

Duration

As we have seen, stock market downturns are not always followed by a recession. However, stock-market downturns do have a pattern of overlapping with recessions. Some market downturns are isolated. For example, a recent downturn in the market has been largely concentrated in the communications and technology sectors; other stocks remain relatively unaffected. Such drops are rarely completely isolated though: other companies' stocks might drop if they themselves have invested in communications and technology companies, or if they are owned by companies also owning affected companies.

Consumer Price Index

The Consumer Price Index (CPI)—an accurate and comprehensive measurement of price fluctuations over long periods of time—is a leading economic indicator. The CPI measures the overall price change over time on a fixed, representative, basket of goods and services. It records price changes in food and beverages, housing, apparel, transportation, entertainment, education, personal care and tobacco products. The CPI can help determine when a recession is nearing an end. In 1981 and 1990, the CPI began to decline before the respective recessions were officially over, causing a reduction in consumer inflation. In 1981, the CPI decline was associated with cheaper food prices. In 1990, the drop in CPI was due to the drop in demand. The Bureau of Labor

Statistics in the U.S. Department of Labor publishes the CPI monthly. The figures are published in the second or third week of the month immediately following the month to which they refer.

Chapter 2
Debt Management

Whether you are budgeting for yourself or an entire family, a basic understanding of the economy you live in is essential. Knowing where you fall in the big economic picture helps put your money into perspective. The economy constantly undergoes ups and downs, and your personal income will most likely reflect what is occurring in the economy overall. A quick debt-management solution will not necessarily revitalize your bank account if the economy is in a prolonged slump. Budgeting should be part of your lifestyle, so you can maximize your money's value at any stage in a fluctuating economy, and particularly during a recession.

Dispelling the Myths

Budgeting might sound like a compromise to your current quality of life, but it does not really require the drastic change that most people think. Before you begin to create a budget, you must be comfortable with why you are budgeting.

Budgeting is increasingly important in our current economic times, where credit cards are everywhere, sixteen-year-olds have phone bills, and most financial transactions can be conducted over the phone or online.

Technology is wonderful, but by making life easier it has also made it harder to keep track of your money. Many payments can be taken directly from your bank account or added directly onto your credit card, where you risk accumulating interest immediately. In addition, it is shocking how a daily cup of coffee or regular takeout lunches can put a sizeable dent into your budget and eat up money that could be going into investments or savings. Without a budget you cannot maximize your money's potential. You work for your money and your money should work for you.

The first step in financial planning is figuring out what your long- and short-term goals are. It does not matter how unrealistic the goals are: you will modify your budget—or modify your goals—to fit your lifestyle. Your goals might be anything from a down payment on a house or a southern vacation to the extra disposable cash to eat out once a week. Goals are personal. The one goal that should be consistent in the early planning stages of a budget is attaining the peace of mind to know you have room in your budget for upsets caused by circumstances beyond your control. Most budgets map out plans for everyday routines, but life does not fit on a tidy spreadsheet. Many people get thrown off their budgets because they do not allot money to allow for unexpected financial crises. Always keep in mind the desired goal of financial security when creating and following your budget.

It Adds Up

Daily cup of coffee	$390/year
2 pack of cigarettes/day	$2,190 – $3,285/year
1 hardback, 3 paperback books/month	$690/year
Takeout lunch 5 days/week (@$5 -$10/day)	$1,300 – $2,600/year
3 drinks at a bar/week	$780/year
3 six-packs of beer/week	$624/year
Total	**$5,974 – $8,369**

Creating a budget that is effective during a recession is favourable because if you can manage your money well during poor economic times, then budgeting should be easy when the economy rebounds. You do not need a prospering economy to develop a budget, nor do you need a lot of personal income. Many people feel that they cannot begin to budget properly until they have paid off certain debts. While debts should of course be paid off, you do need to maintain a certain quality of life, and there are some costs that just cannot be avoided, like food, rent, and mortgage payments. An effective working budget will include strategies for debt management to account for existing financial obligations.

Budgeting

Keep in mind that budgeting is not the same as saving: saving is clipping coupons, but budgeting might involve a change to your lifestyle.

The Don'ts of Budgeting during a Recession

Don't borrow to finance your lifestyle. Adjust your lifestyle to fit what you can afford.

Budgeting should not inflict major changes upon your quality of life, but you must be realistic. If the economy is hurting, your money situation will probably suffer as well. Adjust your spending accordingly; because borrowing to keep yourself in a certain lifestyle is like trying to swim against the economic wave.

Don't buy large-ticket items.

If the economy is in a slump, hold off on buying items such as cars, boats, or even high-priced investments. Even if you have the money, it is safer, in uncertain times, to take the time to watch where the economy is heading.

Don't be too pessimistic ... or optimistic.

As history shows, recessions in the current economy are not the major crises they once were. Pay attention to indicators, and keep an educated degree of optimism in the stock market, rather than pessimism.

The Dos of Creating a Recession-ready Budget

List Expenses.

Figure out what you have to work with by keeping track of *all* your expenses for four weeks. Expenses include everything, even the items that don't seem to be fixed or predictable, such as birthday presents, dinners out, an activation fee. There will always be something that comes up each month that costs a little extra. Overestimating is better than underestimating your expenses.

List income.

Figure out your entire income. Include salaries, interest on savings or investments, stock dividends, and bonuses.

Sort expenses.

Sort your expenses into two groups: fixed and flexible. Fixed expenses are things like mortgages and rent, insurance (car, house, health, life), taxes, and debt repayment. Flexible expenses include groceries, utilities, personal care, and entertainment.

Create a budget.

Your goal in creating a budget is to save up the equivalent of three months of total (fixed and flexible) expenses. Any money saved after that can be put into a more specific savings plan, such as a vacation fund or a particular investment.

Evaluate your Budget

If your debts are not large, take a look at the expenses in your budget and see if you can cut costs somewhere and make higher payments on your debt. It is surprising to learn how quickly debts that are relatively small (a few thousand dollars, for example) become large debts when interest accumulates over time. You do not want to compromise the quality of your life too much, but the freedom of living debt-free is worth making sacrifices for a short period of time to pay off small debts. If your debts are too overwhelming to manage with simple cost-cutting strategies (or if it seems you need more discipline to pay back even small debts), get the pen and paper out again, and create a debt-management plan.

Paying Down Debts

The Don'ts of Paying Down Debt during a Recession

Do not carry your credit cards with you.

Leaving your credit cards at home will help you avoid impulse buying. The time it takes to travel home and get your credit cards will help you think about whether you really need the item or if you just wanted the item. If the item is a necessity, then you can go back home and get your credit card.

Don't use credit cards for consumable items

Don't use credit cards for consumable items such as groceries if you are not making regular payments on your credit card debt. Food is a recurring expense, and should not be a source of debt.

Don't accept or request credit limit increases.

More credit leads to more debt.

Five Steps to Paying Down Small Debt

1. List your debts.

You may think you know who you owe money to and how much, but writing all your debts down on a piece of paper will help you to see all your little debts as one big debt. If you have a collection of credit cards, loans, and other sources of borrowed income, you might sometimes feel like you are constantly having to make payments. Listing your debts will help you focus on one large debt, which may not seem as overwhelming as a bunch of small debts. Start by listing each of your creditors on separate pieces of paper. Add the amount of money owed to each creditor.

2. Reorganize your debts.

Reorganize your debts on another list according to which debts have the highest interest rates (credit cards usually have the highest interest rates). Decide how much you can pay back and try to schedule weekly or monthly payments.

3. Consolidate on your own.

If you can obtain a loan or a line of credit with a low interest rate, you can consolidate your debts on your own. Paying one large debt will help you realize the magnitude of your debt. It will be easier to make payments on this debt, and will save you money on interest charges, if the loan has a low rate. If you avoid the pitfalls of debt consolidation, and resist using the loan as disposable income, then a loan like this can prove very successful.

4. Make a payment plan and stick to it.

You know your own spending habits best. Devise a plan that will allow you to contribute to your debt payments on a weekly or monthly basis. Sticking to the schedule requires discipline, so prepare yourself to commit to the plan until *all* your debts are repaid.

5. Monitor.

If any changes in your income occur, adjust your payments accordingly.

Three Steps to Paying Down Large Debt

You are reading this section because you are in serious debt. The most important part of a debt-payment plan is accepting that you have incurred debt, then realizing that developing a payment plan takes patience, and following a payment plan takes discipline. Start building your confidence by making payments on your debts now. Your plan will take time to develop, and it is helpful to start making consistent payments as soon as possible, to create an awareness of how debt repayment will fit into your life. To set up a debt payment plan, follow these steps:

Step 1: Part A – Organize your debts

List your debts and your creditors. Allot one sheet of paper per debt. List the name of the creditor and how much you owe at the top of each page. Begin to fill in the following information:

- Creditor's address, phone number andfax number
- Creditor's e-mail address or Web site
- Your account number
- Monthly payments
- Interest rate
- Amount and date of last payment made
- Amount and date of next payment due
- Collateral (any assets used to secure debts)
- Name of collection agency or attorney.
- Any legal action already taken

Step 1: Part B – Prioritize

When you begin to figure out how you are going to manage your debts, you may find you do not have enough money to start paying back all of your debts at once, even with a payment plan. It is a good idea to prioritize your debts early on, so you are not overwhelmed by potential expenses. Prioritizing helps you take care of debts one by one, giving attention to the debts that are most crucial first.

Debts that should be at the top of the pile include mortgage or rent, utilities, secured loans (such as car loans), and insurance. Next on your list should be credit cards and debts to finance companies (if these are unsecured debts). Lower-priority debts could include those to doctors and dentists, or hospital bills. Debts to family members and friends should be at the bottom of the list, because they are usually willing to wait the longest.

There are some exceptions. If a creditor is threatening to garnish your wages, you should make a payment on that debt immediately—a loan company can repossess your vehicle, but a doctor cannot take back services already rendered. Therefore, if there is not enough money to make payments on both bills, pay the loan company first, so you can keep your automobile. Put the doctor's bills on hold temporarily, but notify the doctor of your plans and your intention to pay.

Step 2: Set realistic payment goals

Figure out how much you can pay to each of your creditors each month. Then figure out how long it will take for you to eliminate each debt. Add the estimated length of debt repayment to your documentation.

As a general rule, about 75% of an individual's

income is needed to maintain necessary daily living expenses. In light of this, make your payment goals realistic, otherwise you will not stick to them. A reasonable amount to contribute to your debt payments is 20% of your net monthly income. If your debts are very high or numerous, you may want to set aside 25% of your monthly pay for repayments.

A family earning $1500 a month has $300 to put towards debt payments. That leaves $1200 for basic expenses including savings for emergencies. If the family owes $400 a month in payments, then steps must be taken to earn that extra $100.

Making more money

You find that your debt payments are nearly covered by setting aside 20% of your monthly income. In order to stick to your budget, you only need to increase the funds you have on hand for repayment by a small amount. How do you earn a little bit of extra money?

Cut costs

This is where clipping coupons may come in handy. If you are close to your payment goals, trimming costs will make a difference. Many households carry unnecessary costs in the form of extra cable channels, magazine subscriptions, luxury grocery items, or phone accessories.

Earn additional income

Get a part-time job. A second job does not necessarily mean working behind a fast-food counter. You probably have skills that you don't even consider profitable. Think of any skill you might have: carpentry, painting, proofreading, baby-sitting, automotive repair. Start to trumpet your skills so friends and co-workers become aware of what you are capable of and that you are for hire. You could also save money by doing jobs around your own house, like painting instead of hiring others to paint for you.

Sell assets

Review your possessions. Is there anything that you could part with? Do you have an old television set, an extra VCR, jewelry?

Step 3: Set up a plan for paying back your debts

Now that you have figured out how much you owe and to whom, and how much you can pay back, you can begin to figure out *how*, realistically, to pay it back. Your payments can be made using two methods: giving all your creditors equal amounts each month, or paying your creditors in relation to the amount you owe in total. With all methods of payment, your goal is to clear up your debts within three years.

Method A

You pay each creditor an equal amount, regardless of the total value of the debt.

Debt	Amount Owed	Amount Required	Amount You Can Pay
Car loan	$2,000	$200	$75
Bank card	$400	$24	$75
Bank loan#1	$600	$150	$75
Bank loan#2	$900	$200	$75
Total	$3,900	$575	$300

If the total amount available from your monthly

income for debt repayment is $300, you pay each creditor an equal amount: $300 divided by 4 equals $75 per month.

Method B

You determine what proportion of your total debt is represented by each individual debt, and divide your available monthly repayment sum accordingly.

Debt	Amount Owed	% of Total Debt	Amount You Can Pay
Car loan	$2,000	51	$153
Bank card	$400	10	$30
Bank loan#1	$600	16	$48
Bank loan#2	$900	23	$69
Totals	$3,900	100	$300

To determine the percentage of you total debt represented by each separate debt, divide each separate debt by the total amount of debt. Multiply that number by 100 to determine the percentage each debt occupies in your total debt.

For example, your car loan debt is $2,000. Divide that by your total debt ($3,900).

$$\$2,000/\$3,900 = 0.51$$
$$\times 100 = 51\%$$

Your car loan debt represents 51% of your total debt.

To determine the amount that you should pay back per debt each month, multiply the total amount you have set aside for debt repayment by each of the percentages.

Let's use the car loan example again:

$$\$300 \times 0.51 = \$153$$

You can pay back $153 a month on your car loan.

Step 4: Discuss your plan with creditors

Contact each of your creditors. Set up a time to meet with them individually and explain that you have a plan to pay back your debts. Your creditors do not need to know how much you are paying other creditors or who the other creditors are. However, be honest about how many creditors you are in debt to; lying can come back to haunt you later.

Creditors would rather receive a small payment from you than nothing at all. If you cannot pay back the minimum monthly sums they request, explain to your creditors up front why you can not keep up with the payments. Admitting poor money-management skills is a valid reason. Tell your creditor what your income is and show them your plans to pay back the debt month to month.

Consider developing a prorated payment plan to show your creditors. If you need $574 for debt repayment each month, but can only afford $287, you will only be able to pay half of the amount you owe your creditors each month. You can offer each creditor a portion of the debt owed to them. This is called a prorated payment.

Debts	Amount Owed	Amount Required	Prorated Payment
Car loan	$2,000	$200	$100
Bank card	$400	$24	$12
Bank loan	$600	$150	$75
Bank loan	$900	$200	$100
Totals	**$3,900**	**$574**	**$287**

Do not wait for your creditors to contact you about payment plans; they will be more likely to agree to work with you on a payment schedule if you approach them first.

Credit Counseling

A credit counselor negotiates with your creditors for you. A counselor will evaluate your debt situation and draw up a proposal to present to your various creditors. You pay a monthly fee to the counselor, who manages your debts and even makes payments for you. A personal payment plan sounds easy to draw up on paper, but payment plans require discipline, and some people just don't have the willpower or the time to follow their own plans. Credit counselors can provide you with the discipline to get rid of your debts.

A misconception that prevents some people from seeking credit counseling is that it will affect your credit rating. In fact, most credit counseling services do not report to the credit bureau. Future creditors may take note of the use of a counseling service; this is not likely, but it does happen. Having used a counseling service does not weigh nearly as heavily on your credit rating as missed payments or declaring bankruptcy, so you are well-advised to seek help if you need it.

Non-profit vs. for-profit agencies

You will sometimes see credit counseling companies advertised as "non-profit." The difference between non-profit and for-profit companies is usually in the retainer fee required and the interest rates charged. Non-profit companies charge very little, if anything at all, for their services. They never ask for a retainer, although they may ask for a one-time initial fee equal to your first monthly payment. Non-profit companies make money by receiving a small percentage of the total monthly debts that they help settle from creditors (around 10%). The downfall to non-profit companies is that non-profit agencies will sometimes have a higher monthly fee than regular agencies. For-profit agencies will usually ask clients for a retainer or a first payment. The advantages to for-profit agencies are that they may have lower monthly fees and can devote more personal attention to your case. Be aware, though, that not all debts are negotiable. Debts that are non-negotiable include student loans, payments to Revenue Canada, selected credit union loans, many department store accounts, and foreign creditors.

Resources

Listed below are three good resources for those seeking credit counseling.

Debtors Anonymous

Debtors Anonymous was founded in 1968, and is designed for the person whose debts, low income production, and/or "problem spending" are causing suffering. Their members' objective is "... to live without incurring any unsecured debt one day at a time and to help other compulsive debtors to achieve solvency." Today, there are over 500 Debtors Anonymous groups throughout the United States and in 13 other countries as well as on the Internet.

If you are unable to locate a Debtors Anonymous group in your area, you can contact:

General Service Office
P.O. Box 920888
Needham, MA 02492-0009

The organization can also be reached by phone at 781-453-2743 or by e-mail at *new@debtorsanonymous.org.* Their Web site offers links to online Debtors Anonymous groups.

Consumer Credit Counseling Service (CCCS)

The CCCS is the oldest credit-counseling service in America. It is a non-profit organization that helps individuals or families with serious financial problems with budget planning, money management, and planned debt reduction. The counseling service is free, but there is a nominal administrative charge. The CCCS funds itself through the fees that creditors and banks pay to the organization when creditors collect a payment from you.

The CCCS is part of the larger umbrella company called the National Foundation for Consumer Credit (NFCC). You can locate a CCCS organization near you by calling 1-800-388-2227. Be prepared to fill out an application that will be reviewed by a credit counselor.

Myvesta.org

Myvesta.org, formerly known as Debt Counselors of America (DCA), is a debt management organization that provides services for free or at a low cost. Along with debt-management counseling and budgeting, Myvesta.org also offers:

- numerous online and offline articles and publications;

- a financial planning group with certified counselors;

- a Crisis Relief Team to assist those who have been turned down by other agencies or who have significant and complex financial problems; and

- a live radio broadcast with consumer call-ins.

Myvesta.org can be reached at 1-800-680-3328.

In Canada

In Canada, *www.canlaw.com/credit/counselling.htm.* is a resource that has been created by a legal firm and which provides links to credit counseling services in each province.

Other Alternatives

If your debts are high and your creditors will not accept the reduced payments you offer them, then you may have to consider loan consolidation or even bankruptcy.

Loan Consolidation

Loan consolidation involves a loan that will enable you to pay all of your creditors. You will be left with the same total amount of debt, but only one creditor, which means one payment. This solution still requires a great amount of discipline because you still need to find the money to make regular payments. A problem with loan consolidation is that when you consolidate your debts, interest charges on the single debt are high because of the size of the new debt. The consolidation loan should have a lower interest rate than any of your previous debts, however, which means a lower monthly minimum payment. You must pay more than the minimum if you consolidate your debt, though; otherwise you will end up paying more in interest than you would have if your loans remained separate. Consolidation loans are available from many banks, trust companies, credit unions and other financial institutions.

Bankruptcy

Bankruptcy should only be considered after all your other options have been exhausted. Filing for bankruptcy has become increasingly common in recent years, especially among consumers. The stigma associated with bankruptcy seems to be fading, making it a viable option for more and more people. With the high divorce rate, easily available credit, the expansion of legalized gambling and widespread advertising by bankruptcy attorneys, bankruptcy filings are on the rise. Procedures for filing for bankruptcy differ in the United States and Canada.

Bankruptcy in the United States

Bankruptcy is a federal court process that relieves a person or a business of certain debt obligations. There are two main types of bankruptcy arrangements available: reorganization and liquidation.

Reorganization (Chapter 13)

Reorganization is also known as a Chapter 13 bankruptcy. Under this arrangement, you agree to a payment schedule determined by the court, and you are allowed to keep most of your assets. You must report all your debts to the court, even if there are debts that you are still planning on paying off independently; to omit a debt from your payment schedule is a violation of the law. The court protects you from creditor harassment and subsequent legal action while you make monthly payments to a court-appointed trustee, who distributes the payments to your creditors.

This form of bankruptcy may be your only option if your debt load is compiled from debts that cannot be forgiven. Debts like this include child support and alimony, student loans, fines resulting from death or injury caused while driving under the influence of drugs or alcohol, most tax debts, and fines for criminal charges.

In taking responsibility for your debt, you are given more flexibility to pay off your debts. There are some restrictions to Chapter 13 bankruptcy, however:

• You must have most of your debts paid off within three to five years

• You must have a regular income

• You must remain in consistent contact with the court for three to five years. In other words, you cannot move around the country a lot.

•You may not qualify for Chapter 13 bankruptcy if your debt is too high. You cannot owe more than $250,000 in unsecured debts (eg. most credit-card debt) and no more than $750,000 in secured debts (eg. mortgage or car loans).

If you proceed with a Chapter 13 bankruptcy, the consequences are severe; your bankruptcy will tarnish your credit rating for seven to ten years.

Liquidation (Chapter 7)

Liquidation is also known as Chapter 7 bankruptcy. Under this type of bankruptcy, a trustee is appointed by the court to liquidate all or most of your assets. Certain assets cannot be taken away from you; each state has its own regulations as to what you are entitled to keep when you file for bankruptcy and what must be liquidated. There is always a limit to the value of the assets that you can keep. The Bankruptcy Resource Center Web site has links to each Federal District Bankruptcy Code, where you can learn the asset-liquidation guidelines for the region where you live (*www.bankruptcy-resource-center.com/federal-district-bankruptcy-court.htm*).

With the money made from liquidating your assets, your bankruptcy trustee begins to make payments to your creditors. In return, you are absolved of most of your debts. As under Chapter 13, there are certain debts that cannot be absolved: these debts include child support and alimony payments, outstanding debts from a previous bankruptcy, tax debts, certain student loans, and debt resulting from fraud.

Filing for bankruptcy leaves a huge stain on your credit rating that will not be removed for seven to ten years; this will hinder your chances of rebuilding your financial standing with the help of loans.

What are the benefits of filing for bankruptcy?

Immediately after you file for bankruptcy, all actions against you by creditors or collection agencies are halted. Any lawsuits pending against you relating to your debt are stopped. This is called an "automatic stay," under which you must work only through the court exclusively to pay off your debts. An automatic stay allows you to buy time with a number of your creditors such as your utility company; you will be given at least twenty days to pay off your account before your utilities can be disconnected. An automatic stay can also stop foreclosure on your house. In a Chapter 7 bankruptcy, though, a foreclosure cannot be prevented for long before the creditor insists that the stay be removed. Likewise, if you are renting, an automatic stay buys you a few extra days or weeks before you can be legally evicted. The stay also prevents the IRS from issuing a tax lien. In a Chapter 13 bankruptcy, the stay stops interest from accruing on your tax debts. As soon as the bankruptcy case is closed, the stay is terminated and you are subject to all actions taken by creditors thereafter.

The Bankruptcy Process in the United States

Filing

Before you file for bankruptcy, speak to a lawyer and decide which type of bankruptcy arrangement you should opt for. The next step is to complete legal forms that list your assets and debts; these forms will then be presented to the court. If the court approves your bankruptcy petition, your lawyer will meet with your creditors to assess your debts. Depending on whether you file Chapter 13 or Chapter 7, your lawyer and creditors will either liquidate your assets or develop a payment schedule.

Approximately sixty days after you file, you will have to appear in court and discuss your intentions with regard to your debts with your lawyer, your creditors, and a court-appointed trustee. The trustee will also review the effect that bankruptcy will have on your credit history and legal rights. After your court appearance, your creditors will have sixty days to object to the arrangements that the court has made to discharge your debts. The court will then review the arguments and determine which debts to discharge.

Obtaining a Lawyer

If you don't know where to find a bankruptcy lawyer, contact your local bar association. It can refer you to a lawyer who will be able to help you free of charge if you can't afford to pay legal fees. Alternatively, you can contact a legal-aid service or a university law school with a legal-assistance program for inexpensive or free legal services. Make sure that the lawyer you settle on is state-certified or certified in bankruptcy practice. Also keep in mind that your lawyer needs to know everything about your finances, so be sure that you're comfortable with him or her.

In order to file for a Chapter 7 or Chapter 13 bankruptcy, you must pay a fee of $175. This fee is set under federal regulations and is the same in all states.

Bankruptcy in Canada

In Canada, bankruptcy is a legal proceeding available to people in a financial crisis. The purpose of bankruptcy is to allow those hopelessly burdened with debt to have a "new lease on life." A person must be insolvent in order to file for bankruptcy. To be insolvent involves owing at least $1,000 to creditors and being unable meet your debts as they are due to be paid.

Types of bankruptcy

Proposal under the Payment of Debts System

Without officially filing for bankruptcy, you can file a proposal with your province's Payment of Debts System. This is similar to Chapter 13 bankruptcy in the United States because it grants you an extension on your debt repayment free from harassment from creditors for a specified time period.

Proposal under the Bankruptcy and Insolvency Act

Under this arrangement, you are assigned a trustee who files a proposal with your creditors to absolve you of some of your debts and gives you an extension on payments. The proposal is generally only accepted if the creditors stand to gain more by giving you a partial discharge rather than have you go completely bankrupt and not pay your creditors anything. This type of proposal has a very high acceptance rate.

Bankruptcy

When you file for bankruptcy in Canada, you give up your assets to a trustee who liquidates them and begins payments to your creditors. If you are a first-time filer for bankruptcy, you can be discharged from your debts within nine months. The bankruptcy stays on your credit rating, however, for the following six years. You are also required to seek credit counseling during your bankruptcy. The debts that cannot be discharged with any kind of bankruptcy in Canada are:

- Fines imposed by a court

- Money owing for stolen goods

- Goods obtained through misrepresentation

- Alimony or maintenance payments

- Fines awarded by a court for inflicting bodily harm or sexual assault

- Student loans if the bankruptcy is filed prior to or within ten years of finishing school

Assets that cannot be liquidated during the bankruptcy process differ from province to province. Below is a list of what assets you get to keep depending on where you live in Canada.

Alberta
Clothing – $ 4,000; Household Goods – $4,000; Tools of the Trade – $10,000; Farmers – enough supplies to survive next twelve months; Motor Vehicle – $ 5,000; Principal Residence – $ 40,000

British Columbia
Vehicle – $5,000; Household Goods – $4,000; Tools of the Trade – $10,000; Principal Residence – between $9,000 and $12,000

Manitoba
Clothing – six months' worth or cash equivalent;

Household Goods – $4,500; Tools of the Trade – $7,500; Farmers – enough supplies to survive next twelve months; Motor Vehicle – $3,000; Principal Residence – $1500 per joint tenant or $2500 if there is only one tenant

New Brunswick

Vehicle – $6,500; Household Goods – $5,000; Tools of the Trade – $6,500; Clothing – as necessary for survival

Newfoundland

Clothing – $4,000; Household Goods – $4,000; Tools of the Trade – $7,500; Sentimental Goods – $500; Property for Income – $10,000; Principal Residence – $10,000

Nova Scotia

Clothing – as necessary for survival; Household Goods – as necessary for survival; Tools of the Trade – $1,000; Vehicle – $3,000

Ontario

Clothing – $5,000; Household Goods – $10,000; Tools of the Trade – $10,000; Farmers – $25,000; Motor Vehicle – $ 5,000

Quebec

Clothing – as necessary for survival; Household Goods – $6,000

Saskatchewan

Non-farmers

Principal Residence – $32,000 ($64,000 if jointly

owned); Household Goods – $4,500; Tools of the Trade – $4,500; Vehicle – if required for employment

Farmers

Clothing – as necessary for survival; Household Goods – $10,000; Tools of the Trade – $4,500; Farmers – enough supplies to survive next twelve months; Principal Residence – $32,000 ($64,000 if jointly owned)

The Bankruptcy Process in Canada

If you file for bankruptcy in Canada, you must keep your trustee informed as to where you are living, must respond to your trustee's requests, assist your trustee as required, and provide him or her with whatever information is requested. You keep your trustee up to date about what you are earning, what your living expenses are and any changes in your family situation. A meeting of creditors is not required unless requested by the Superintendent of Bankruptcy or creditors with an aggregate of at least 25% of the proven claims. Fees for the trustee, administration, and counseling related to your bankruptcy are regulated by the government. A trustee is usually paid from the funds accumulated from the liquidation of the bankrupt person's assets. If there are no assets, the bankrupt person will be required to pay the trustee's fees over time.

Rebuilding Your Credit Rating

Whether you've filed for bankruptcy or have accumulated a significant debt load, it takes seven years for bad credit to be absolved from your credit rating. You may not have any big purchases in mind right now, but try and think ahead seven years to a time when you might be seeking a significant line of credit.

A copy of your credit rating is free (or available for a very nominal fee). Don't be surprised if your credit rating is lower than you expect; credit companies have records of all your missed or late payments. In Canada and the United States you can contact one of three sources to obtain a free credit rating:

Equifax Information Services, LLC
P.O. Box 740241
Atlanta, GA 30374
www.equifax.com/1-800-685-1111

TransUnion LLC
Consumer Disclosure Center
P.O. Box 1000
Chester, PA 19022
www.tuc.com/1-800-888-4213

Experian
www.experian.com/1-888-EXPERIAN (397-3742)

If you find anything that looks like a discrepancy or an error on your credit rating, write to the credit bureau that supplied the report and request a correction, enclosing copies of documents that would establish proof of an error.

Your credit rating is determined by three major factors: credit use, length of employment, and length of residency. You can improve your rating whether or not you are in debt, by showing a responsible use of credit. If your bank won't issue you a credit card or allow you to open a savings account, you may obtain a "secured" credit card. With a secured credit card you deposit funds with a particular creditor before you are issued the credit card. There are usually steep application and annual fees applied, as well as higher than average interest rates. Remember that fees and interest rates vary, so shop around before selecting a secured creditor. You cannot contribute anything but time and effort to the other major factors affecting your credit rating—your length of residency and length of employment. Just be aware, when choosing to move or to leave a job, of the effects these actions may have on your rating.

Chapter 3
Job Security and Retention

During a recession, some companies and industries are more susceptible to economic downturns than others; therefore, certain types of firms are more likely to lay off their employees as a way of dealing with declining revenues.

Cyclical Businesses

Some businesses are cyclical by nature. A good example of this is the car industry. When times are prosperous, people buy large-ticket items like cars in sizable numbers. When there is a downturn, however, and people become uncertain about their future, they tend to put off purchasing large-ticket items. The result is that the automobile industry and others like it experience great fluctuations in their sales that reflect the state of the overall economic environment.

Other types of businesses are not affected by the rise and fall of financial expectations to the same degree. Industries and businesses dealing in products or services that people have to buy regardless of whether a recession is happening or not—food producers and discount retailers, for example—generally don't experience the dramatic ups and downs in revenue that car manufacturers do.

Heavy Debt Loads

Companies that are carrying heavy debt loads are particularly susceptible to economic downturns. These organizations are required to fulfill obligations to their creditors while their revenues may well be declining. Corporate debt repayment is difficult to restructure; so companies often look for other ways to reduce expenditures during tough economic periods. They might consider reducing overall production or reducing their payrolls to trim fat from their budgets. Furthermore, a company's creditors might be in difficult financial straits themselves and demand debt repayment immediately. Carrying a heavy debt load gives a company less maneuvering room to deal with new economic conditions.

Warning Signs

When the dark clouds of a recession appear on the economic horizon, businesses start looking for ways to cut expenses and prepare for lean times to come. There are a number of warning signs that suggest that downsizing may be part of the recession-survival plan for a particular company.

Negative Media

If you're reading articles in the media about a bearish market and an economic slowdown and hearing pessimistic commentaries about the future, so are your bosses and the investors in your business. Your particular company may not be feeling the crunch yet, but its management will be very aware of the general business environment and will be thinking about what might be done to lessen the effects of an economic downturn.

Layoffs at Competitors', Suppliers' & Customers' Firms

If your company's competitors, suppliers and/or customers are downsizing, it is certain that your company will be examining the possibility as well because this shows that the recession is affecting your industry. Your company has to remain competitive to survive, and its strategy most certainly involves keeping expenses in check to maintain its financial viability. If a competing company is making the same product as yours at a lower cost due to a reduction in its work force, your company is going to be in trouble.

Layoffs also provide an indication of what people in your industry think will happen. They expect that they will not be able to generate as much money as they once did, and this becomes a self-fulfilling prophecy. If your customers are laying people off, you can be pretty sure that they will not be willing to spend as much to purchase your company's products and services in the near future.

Earning Warnings

As firms anticipate a recession and begin to expect less revenue, publicly traded companies in your industry will start to issue earning warnings to their investors. They are preparing their investors for the downturn by admitting that the company won't be making as much as money in the near future, and that its investors should be prepared to expect a reduction in dividends.

Budget cuts

In a recessionary period, your company's management will be required to cut its budget in an effort to reduce expenses.

Project Cancellations or Suspensions

New projects within your company may be canceled or put on the back burner so that the firm's resources can be directed to its core operations, reducing the risks associated with new ventures.

Management Resignations

Sometimes difficult economic times are characterized by a power struggle within an organization's management. Arguments arise over whose department to cut, and by how much, and this can become a point of friction within the management group. Occasionally these disputes will cause members of upper management to resign.

Termination of Temps and Contractors

One of the easiest ways for a company to reduce expenditures is to terminate temporary positions and contractors. Usually management is not encumbered by collective agreements that bind these positions and the workers who occupy them to the company. Temps and contractors are also the easiest positions to eliminate, because their work is not usually tied as closely to the core business of the company as that of full-time employees.

Downsizing

There are three kinds of company downsizing: work-force reduction, work redesign and systemic downsizing.

Work-force Reduction

Companies looking for a quick-fix solution to their economic woes may choose a work-force reduction. The goal is to reduce the number of people on the payroll. This is done in a few different ways:

1) Attrition

Work-force attrition means that when an employee leaves a position, no one is hired to replace them.

2) Layoffs

A company may decide to take a more drastic approach and lay off people wholesale throughout the organization. Layoffs can be temporary or permanent.

3) Buy-out packages

To reduce its number of employees, a company may offer financial incentives (buy-out packages) to employees to encourage them to leave the firm voluntarily.

A work-force reduction is a top-down directive determined by a company's management group, and produces short-term benefits. This strategy is usually implemented quickly, in the hope of minimizing disturbance to the organization.

Sometimes this strategy is also meant to highlight to remaining employees the seriousness of the financial situation the organization faces. It is hoped that employees will be more efficient and adaptable in their job performance, as well as more willing to accept changes in the workplace that might make the organization more profitable or productive.

There are some disadvantages to this strategy. The results of this kind of downsizing are very unpredictable. Managers cannot predict with any accuracy who will take advantage of offered buy-out packages. In addition, it is difficult to tell what organizational memory and critical skills will be lost when certain employees leave. Finally, downsizing in general creates low employee morale and infects the corporate environment with anxiety.

Work Redesign

The goal of work redesign is reducing the amount of work performed overall with a company, rather than necessarily reducing the number of people performing the work. This strategy can involve eliminating certain levels of hierarchy in management, merging departments or work groups, redesigning work, limiting the number of hours certain employees work, or ending production of labor-intensive products.

This strategy cannot be carried out effectively on a short-term basis, because it requires much analysis of what can and should be eliminated or merged. If administered appropriately, however, it can greatly increase an organization's efficiency.

Systemic Downsizing

This type of long-term downsizing focuses on changing an organization's culture and the attitudes of its employees. Downsizing is not just a set target or an isolated project but becomes a way of life; it is an ongoing process aimed at continuously improving efficiency. Employees are held responsible for saving the organization money. All aspects of the organization—from suppliers, inventories, design processes and production methods, to customer relations, marketing and sales support—

are examined for the possibility of saving. Costs throughout the organization are the targets of this kind of downsizing. Instead of being the first targets for elimination, employees are viewed as resources, capable of helping to generate and implement efficiency ideas.

These three types of downsizing strategies are not mutually exclusive; often companies will implement two or more of these strategies at the same time.

Surviving an Uncertain Employee Environment

1. Understand your industry

Knowledge of the industry and its outlook are essential to survival. Read industry reports and pay attention to financial news. There are online publications relating to virtually every industry. As well, speak to colleagues in your field. Ask your boss how industry developments will affect your company and your job. You will gain valuable insight into what investors and industry analysts are saying about your company's ability to survive.

2. Research your company

Find out how your company is doing financially— whether sales are up or down compared to previous years and whether the company is profitable or not. This information will allow you to evaluate your company's need to downsize. If your employer is a public company, you can obtain the same information investors do, including analysts' reports. Learn to read the company's quarterly report and balance sheet; it will tell you exactly how profitable the company has been during the last three months. Financial analysts' reports can hint at whether the company is under pressure to reduce costs and possibly downsize.

3. Find out where your job fits in the company

Examine whether your job and your department are essential parts of the core business of the organization. Also consider whether your department and ultimately your job are profitable. Managers examine these things when deciding what departments and positions to cut. One indication that your department is a target for reduction is that it has not received consistent financial or staffing support from the management. If you suspect that your department is a target for job cuts, attempt to transfer to a department that is essential or profitable. Upgrade your skills or add new ones that are applicable to other areas of the organization; this will make it easier to parachute into a safer area.

4. Be a team player

Avoid conflict with fellow employees and managers and focus on doing the best job you can do. All things being equal, when managers are determining which employees to lay off they will first think of those who tend to create problems for them and the rest of their staff.

5. Become an expert in what your company or department doesn't do well

Examine the situations that your department has difficulty dealing with and come up with ways of solving these problems. Become the resident expert in these areas, and you make yourself essential to your department.

6. Look for ways to save your company money

If you determine new ways to save time and money, you will be seen as someone who can aid your organization in difficult financial times. This skill is also highly valuable to any manager who is trying to shepherd his or her department through the quagmire of cost cutting.

7. Build a professional relationship with your boss's boss

Make an effort to communicate with your boss's boss and to develop some kind of professional relationship. Putting a face to your name and establishing your presence with the next level of management means that it will be more difficult for them to give you the axe.

8. Don't screw up

Be additionally attentive to your work: mistakes cost your company money, and during a recessionary period management will be watching every penny. It is important not to give your manager reasons to lay you off.

If You Get Laid Off

There are no guarantees in life, and despite your best efforts you may be laid off. What do you do?

Understand your rights to benefits

Find out what your rights to benefits are. Some of these rights may be outlined in an employee handbook, if you have one; state, provincial and federal laws guarantee others. Generally, the law requires that employers pay employees for work already performed. Some jurisdictions also require employers to pay employees for unused vacation time at an termination of employment. Federal laws also guarantee health and pension benefits when an employee loses his or her job. If your company is shutting down altogether or laying off large numbers of employees, you may be entitled to sixty days' notice with pay—federal laws require certain employers employing 100 or more people to provide a sixty-day advance notice of the layoff. If an employer violates the law, it can be required to pay employees back pay for the period of the notification. Employees can also file complaints with the U.S. Department of Labor Employment or Employment Canada. Contact your local department of labor to find out more about your rights under state or provincial law.

Unemployment

Losing your job is not the end of the world; it may be a way for new opportunities to materialize for you. Here are some tips for a job search:

1. Keep getting up in the morning. Maintaining a routine will help you keep your spirits up and allow you to maximize your efforts in finding another job.

2. Contact the unemployment office nearest you immediately to sign up for unemployment-insurance benefits and to search for new jobs.

3. Update and polish your resume.

4. Start searching for a new job right away.

5. Submit your updated resume to job sites on the Internet, to let employers come to you.

6. Apply to receive e-mail notification of new jobs at sites that offer it, to let the jobs come to you, too.

7. Contact your professional references to let them know you're back in the job market and counting on them.

8. Ask your previous boss to write a letter of recommendation for you that includes an explanation that your most recent job loss wasn't your fault.

9. Practice your interview skills while you have the time to keep your confidence level up.

10. Consider temping or doing contract work, if possible, until you find a permanent job.

11. Let your friends, relatives and acquaintances know that you are searching for a new job.

12. To avoid worry and depression, keep your mind busy and make yourself feel useful by working on your house, car, yard and hobbies.

Chapter 4
Investing

Once your basic needs (housing, clothing and food) have been met, you should develop a plan to invest your extra money. But in uncertain economic times, where do you put those hard-earned extra dollars?

One of the most important things to determine before you start investing during an economic downturn is whether the economy is heading into a recession or is beginning to recover from a recession. This will help you decide what kinds of investment vehicles to put your money in. In previous chapters, we looked at what indicators show us that we are heading into a recession. Now we can look at what indicators suggest that the economy is on the road to recovery.

Economic Indicators

Consumers

Consumer spending is the linchpin of the North American economy, and happy consumers spend more than pessimistic ones. There are two reports that measure consumer confidence efficiently: the University of Michigan's Consumer Sentiment Index, released twice a month, and the Conference Board's Consumer Confidence

Survey, released on the last Tuesday of each month.

The Conference Board conducts a monthly survey of 5,000 households to ascertain their level of consumer confidence. The report can be helpful in predicting sudden shifts in consumption patterns, though it also registers smaller changes that are not as significant. The Consumer Confidence Survey consists of two subindexes measuring consumers' appraisal of current economic conditions and their expectations for the future. The expectations index is usually seen as conveying more accurate indicator qualities than the current conditions index. Specifically, the survey gauges respondents' appraisal of current business conditions, their expectations regarding business conditions six months hence, their appraisal of current employment conditions, their expectations regarding employment conditions six months hence and their expectations regarding their total family income six months hence.

The Michigan index is very similar to the Conference Board survey, although there are two monthly releases, a preliminary report and a final reading. Like the Consumer Confidence Survey, it has two subindexes that relate to consumers' expectations and their evaluation of current conditions.

Jobs

Few things make consumers happier than knowing that the labor market is healthy. That's why the Labor Department's employment report, released the first Friday of every month, is worth watching. Look at the change in non-farm payrolls; a good sign of economic rebound is back-to-back monthly increases in non-farm payrolls.

Capital Goods

Infrastructure spending by businesses, particularly spending on equipment, will increase if the economy is on the rebound. The best indicator of this is the national quantity of capital-goods orders, measured as a component of the Census Bureau's durable-goods orders report released at the end of each month. A consistent rise in capital-goods orders indicates that business spending on equipment is on the upswing.

Stock Market Indicators

Momentum

One sign of a bull market is that investors are willing to pay higher prices for stocks. Market analysts watch the 200-day moving average of the Standard & Poor's 500-stock index. To calculate it, add up the closing index prices for the past 200 trading days and divide by 200. When the current price is higher than the average over the past 200 days—and stays that way—it's a bullish sign.

Breadth

A rising market index doesn't mean much if all the gains are in a few stocks. Examine the market's breadth by comparing the daily number of stocks that are gaining in value (advancing issues) to the number of stocks that are losing value (declining issues) on the New York Stock Exchange. In the early stages of bull markets, there is usually one day and sometimes two or three within a few weeks' span when advancing issues are five times more numerous than declining issues.

"Put" and "Call" Options

Examining the trading of "put" and "call" options is one way to determine attitudes among stock-market investors. A call option is a stock-purchasing arrangement that gives the buyer the right to buy a certain quantity (usually 100 shares) of a stock at a specified price up to a specified date. For example, an investor might purchase a call option on General Electric stock that confers the right to buy 100 shares at $25 per share until October 17. Calls are sold to investors for a fee by other investors who incur an obligation.

A put option, on the other hand, is a selling arrangement that gives a stockholder the right to sell a certain quantity of a particular stock at a specified price up to a specified date. For example, an investor might purchase a put option on GenCorp common stock that confers the right to sell 100 shares of his or her stock at $80 per share until September 21. Puts are sold for a fee by other investors, who incur an obligation to purchase the stock if the option holder decides to sell. Investors purchase puts in order to take advantage of a decline in the price of the asset.

Put buyers are bears, call buyers are bulls. When the stock market is hitting bottom, put buyers will outnumber call buyers. An increased frequency of call buys indicates that the market is on its way to recovery.

Stock Market

During an economic downturn, the stock market is the first part of the economy to be affected and also the first to experience recovery (usually halfway through a recession). One of the stock market's primary functions is to anticipate the economy's performance in the future;

that's why the market will recover partway through a recession as investors envision recovery.

As the economy heads into recession, we often see the stock market take a tremendous beating as investors flee from the market in an effort to protect their investments from an expected decline in corporate earnings. Stock values can become disassociated from the economic reality of the companies they represent: a corporation might warn investors that it will not be able to meet its profit projections, and its share prices may plummet, despite the fact that the corporation itself is still a very viable venture, capable of returning profits and with good long-term prospects. In this way, the share price may drop disproportionately given the actual value of the corporation.

In fact, a recession is one of the best times to invest in the stock market, especially if recovery is close. If an investor believes economic recovery is just around the corner, he or she may well invest in growth stocks, such as technology stocks. However, if the same investor believes the economy is entering a recession or that an existing recession is going to be long and severe, a preferable option might be investing in blue-chip stocks such as pharmaceutical or financial companies, since such stocks tend to turn out profits even in hard economic times. There are literally thousands of strategies for investing in the stock market. We will look at a few basics of picking stocks with a recession in mind.

Selecting Stocks

Financial Condition

A simple measure you can use to evaluate the financial condition of a particular company is the current ratio, which is the ratio of its current assets to current liabilities. A very conservative investor would look for a company with current assets that are twice the value of its current liabilities. A somewhat less conservative but relatively safe approach might permit a company's current assets to be only one-and-a-half times its current liabilities. As you would expect, the larger a company's current ratio, the stronger its financial condition.

Earnings and Growth

For a company to be considered a good value, it should show a long history of earnings without losses. Even a few years of positive earnings are better than no earnings at all. At a minimum, a good-value company should have increased its earnings over the previous year. Even better would be several years of continuously improving earnings.

Price of Earnings

The price of earnings refers to how much you must pay for each dollar of earnings a stock generates. A stock that is a good value will have a low price-to-earnings ratio. Let's say that a stock costs $15 for each dollar of earnings it generates. That's a price-to-earnings ratio (P/E ratio) of 15 or less—a good value. A stock with a P/E ratio of less than 10 ($10 for each dollar of earnings) is an even better value.

Price of Assets

To determine whether a certain stock is a good value, compare the stock price to the total value of the company's tangible assets, or compare the stock price to the company's book value (its total assets minus liabilities). Alternatively, you might consider the price-to-book ratio, which is a stock's capitalization divided by its book value. To be a good value, the stock price should not be higher than 150% of the tangible assets, or greater than 150% of book value.

Dividends

Some investors demand that their stocks earn dividends. Others prefer that their investments not pay dividends because of tax consequences: dividends are taxed twice. (Corporations pay tax on their earnings before dividends are distributed, then investors must pay income tax on the dividends they receive.) Dividends are now a matter of personal choice. If you are seeking dividend income to help cover your living expenses, you should look for stocks with a fairly long history of consistent payments.

Size of the Company

While a company of any size can be a good value, larger companies tend to weather economic downturns better than small companies. However, smaller companies tend to recover more quickly than larger ones since they are able to respond more quickly to changes in the economic environment.

Shorting Stocks

There is another way to make money in a bear market, but it is not for the inexperienced investor. This is called shorting a stock, also referred to as "going short" or taking a "short position." Essentially you sell stock you do not own in anticipation of buying the stock to cover the sale later, when the price goes down. Where do you get the stock? You borrow it from your broker. In other words, a short seller sells a security he thinks will fall in value and then waits for the price to fall. If the seller's prediction was correct, he can later buy the security back ("covering the short") at a lower price, closing out, or "covering," his short position for a profit. Short selling is a way to earn profit when the price of a stock drops. Rather than the more common "buy low and sell high" tactic, short sellers "sell high and buy low," or sell low and buy lower.

Thus, if you short sell 1,000 shares of a company at $20 a share, your account with your broker gets credited with $20,000. The stock begins to fall and bottoms out at $8 a share. At this point, you purchase 1,000 shares to "cover your short" and return the shares to your broker. You have made a profit of $12,000.

Sounds good, doesn't it? There is a problem, however: what if the stock goes up in value instead of down? Sometimes companies turn their fortunes around quickly, or the economy as a whole begins to accelerate and correspondingly the share rises in value. You might end up with a scenario like this: you short sell 1,000 shares of a company at $20 a share and your account with your broker gets credited with $20,000. Then the stock begins to take off and you find it is now trading for $47 a share. You decide to cover your short before the stock goes up any more. Since it will cost you $47,000 to purchase the 1,000 shares you need to cover your short, you end up with a loss of $27,000. To add insult to injury, if the stock pays out a dividend while you are shorting, you will have to pay your broker that dividend when you cover the short.

Another thing to consider when short selling is that it is almost guaranteed that you are not the only one shorting any particular stock. Experienced investors will look at which shares have been shorted and in what quantities (the "short interest"). All these shorts will turn into buy orders at some point and may give the astute market watcher an indication of when a particular share is about to rally. Hence, shorting stocks is definitely not for the faint of heart or shallow of pocketbook.

Bonds

A bond is essentially an IOU agreement in which an investor agrees to loan money to a company or government in exchange for interest on their money at a predetermined rate.

As a business grows, a time will come when it does not have enough capital available to pay for all the elements of its own expansion. When this happens, most businesses have two options: they can either sell a portion of the company to the general public by issuing shares, or they can issue bonds. When a company issues bonds, it is borrowing money from investors in exchange for agreeing to pay them interest on their money at a set date in the future. It is the same thing as a mortgage—only you, the investor, are the bank.

Similarly, governments sometimes run into the same problem and do not have enough money to pay for all the services they want to provide to the people under their jurisdiction. Obviously a country, state or province cannot sell a piece of itself to investors, but it can borrow money from individuals by issuing bonds. The face value of a bond is generally $1,000 unless specified otherwise

Benefits of Bonds

While bonds may not produce the sometimes spectacular profits seen on the stock market, they have several traits that stocks simply can't match.

1. Capital preservation

Unless a company goes bankrupt, a bondholder can be almost completely certain that he or she will recover the amount that was originally invested. When investing on the stock market, losing all the money you have invested is not only possible, it happens frequently.

2. Regular payout

Bonds pay interest at set intervals, which can provide valuable income for retired people and others who rely on the cash flow from their investments. Owing $100,000 worth of bonds that paid 8% interest annually, for example, would provide the bond holder with a significant monthly or quarterly sum to live on or invest elsewhere.

3. Tax exemption

Bonds can also carry large tax advantages. When a government or municipality issues bonds to raise funds to build bridges, roads, and so on, the interest that is earned by investors is tax exempt.

Bonds and Risk

Government bonds

National Governments

National governments have the power to print money to pay their debts, as they control the money supply and currency of their countries. This is why most investors consider bonds issued by national governments of most modern industrial countries to be almost risk-free.

Provincial and State Governments

Provincial and state governments also issue bonds, depending upon their constitutional ability to do so. Canadian provinces, Ontario in particular, borrow more than many smaller countries. Most investors consider provincial- or state-issued bonds to be very strong credits because states and provinces maintain the power to levy income and sales taxes to support their debt payments. Such bonds are not quite as secure as those issued by national governments, but they still represent very solid investments.

Municipal and Regional Governments

Cities, towns, counties and regional municipalities issue bonds supported by their property taxes. School boards also issue bonds that are supported by their ability to levy a portion of municipal property taxes for education. Most municipal bonds are sold in denominations of $5,000.

Quasi-Government Issuers

Many government-related institutions issue bonds, some supported by their own revenues and some guaranteed by a government sponsor. In Canada, federal government agencies and Crown corporations issue bonds. Bonds from institutions such as the Federal Business Development Bank (FBDB) and the Canadian Mortgage and Housing Corporation (CMHC) are directly guaranteed by the federal government. Bonds from provincial Crown corporations such as Hydro Quebec are guaranteed by the provinces in which they are issued.

Corporate Bonds

Debt capital is money loaned to corporations by investors; the bond represents the corporation's debt. This is a key difference between a bond and a stock. Stock represents an ownership interest in the company. If you accumulate enough stock, you will own the company, whereas a bond is a loan and you don't own any part of the company. A bond certificate will state the corporation's obligation to pay back a specific amount of money, at a specific point in time, at a specific rate of interest. Interest on corporate bonds is usually paid twice a year. Corporate bonds can be either secured or unsecured. An unsecured bond is backed by the reputation, credit record and financial stability of the issuing corporation. These are generally issued by the largest corporations and are regarded as highly safe. These unsecured bonds are known as debentures.

Bond-related Terms You Should Know

Indenture

The indenture is the legal agreement between the corporation and the party loaning the corporation money. The indenture, which is printed on the bond certificate, contains

   • the duties and obligations of the trustee (usually
   a bank or trust company hired by the corporation);

- all the rights of the lender (the bondholder);

- how and when the principal will be repaid;

- the rate of interest;

- the description of any property to be pledged as collateral;

- steps the bondholder can take in the event of default.

Bearer Bonds

Bearer bonds are also known as coupon bonds. No one's name is on the bond or the coupon; the coupons, which represent the interest the bond is earning, are submitted twice a year to the authorized bank for redemption. A twenty-year bond of $1,000 value paying 8% interest annually would have forty coupons for $40 each. Bearer bonds can be used like cash; they are highly negotiable and there are still many in circulation. However, the Tax Reform Act of 1982 ended the issue of bearer bonds.

Registered Bonds

Today bonds are sold in a fully registered form; they come with your name already on them. Twice a year, you receive a check for the interest the bond earns. When the bond matures, the registered owner receives a check for the principal. A partially registered bond is a cross between a registered bond and a coupon bond: the bond is registered to you as its owner; however, it has coupons attached which you send in to the issuing bank for payment.

Book Entry Bonds

In 1986, all U.S. Government bonds were sold in book entry form. When these bonds are sold, the owner of the bond is not issued a certificate; instead, his or her name is entered in the Federal Reserve Board computer. This computer keeps track of who owns what and when the interest needs to be paid. A growing number of other bonds are now being sold in book entry form.

Return

The return is perhaps the most difficult part of bond investing for most people to understand. There are two factors that affect how high a return a certain bond investment may offer. The first is demand when many companies want to borrow money, the cost of borrowing (the interest rate) goes up. When there is less demand to borrow money, the cost of borrowing (the interest rate) goes down. The second factor that influences the price of a bond is the risk/reward ratio involved. As the risk involved in a particular bond investment increases, investors must be given a higher incentive to buy. Therefore, the riskier the issue, the higher the rate of interest will be.

Nominal Yield

Nominal yield is the interest rate stated on the face of the bond. This is also referred to as the coupon rate. A $1,000 corporate bond with a nominal yield of 10% will pay $100 a year in interest.

Current Yield

Current yield is the annual return in dollars on a particular bond divided by its current market price. Let's say the current market price of a certain bond is $1,200 and its annual return is $100. The current yield is $100 divided by $1,200, or 8.3% (.08333). Regardless of how much the bond changes in price, the nominal yield (interest paid as stated on the face of the bond) always remains the same. However, because bonds fluctuate in price (they are bought and sold like stocks), the return the investor receives fluctuates, and so does the current yield.

Premium and Discount

If a bond is trading for more than its face amount (usually $1,000), it is said to be trading at a premium. If a bond is trading for less than its face value, it is said to be trading at a discount. Therefore, a bond trading at $1,400 is trading at a premium and a bond trading at $700 is trading at a discount. If you buy a bond trading at a premium, you receive a lower return than the one stated on the face of the bond. And if you buy a bond trading at a discount, you receive a higher return than that stated on the face of the bond.

Yield to Maturity or True Yield

When an investor buys a bond that is trading at a price higher or lower than $1,000, he still receives $1,000 in principal repayment when the bond matures. Someone who pays $1,200 for a bond still only receives $1,000 at maturity; a bond bought for $900 is also worth $1,000 when its principal is repaid. The difference between par value (the face value of the bond) and the amount the investor actually paid for the bond is also considered yield and has to be included in yield calculations. In other words, the investor needs to account for this difference in price to better understand what the true value of the bond is. There are two different ways to calculate a bond's yield to maturity. The first is used if the investor bought the bond at a discount. The second calculation is used if the bond was bought at a premium.

Discount Bonds

$$\text{Yield to maturity} = \frac{\text{coupon} + \text{prorated discount}}{(\text{face value} + \text{purchase price}) / 2}$$

Where:

coupon = dollar amount of annual interest

prorated discount = divide the discount by the number of years remaining until maturity to come up with a dollar amount

face value = usually $1,000

purchase price = amount you paid for the bond

Premium Bonds

$$\text{Yield to maturity} = \frac{\text{coupon} - \text{prorated premium}}{(\text{face value} + \text{purchase price}) / 2}$$

Generally, a bond's yield to maturity is what traders consider most closely when evaluating a bond.

Types of Corporate Bonds

There are various types of corporate secured bonds, but the most common are mortgage bonds, equipment trust certificates and income bonds.

Mortgage Bonds

Corporations sometimes issue bonds that are backed by real estate and/or the physical assets of the company.

The real assets pledged on the bonds will have a market value greater than the bond issue; if the company defaults on the bonds, the real assets are sold to pay off the bondholders. There are two types of mortgage bonds:

1. Closed-end Mortgage Bonds
If the mortgage bond you buy is secured with closed-end assets, the assets pledged can only be sold off to pay off your bond issue.

2. Open-end Mortgage Bonds
If, however, you buy a mortgage bond that is pledged with open-end assets, those assets may also be pledged against other bond issues. In case of a default, bond-holders from other issues will have equal claim to those assets.

Equipment Trust Certificates

These bonds function in a manner similar to a car loan. When you borrow money for a new car, you make a down payment, then you make monthly installment payments. At no time throughout the life of the loan is your car worth less than the outstanding amount of the loan. Many railroad and transportation companies finance their operations using this same type of arrangement. Usually, 20% of the purchase price is put down by the company in the form of a down payment. Then the balance is paid off over fifteen years. When the company is finished paying off the loan, it receives clear title from the trustee. If the company defaults on the loan, its equipment is sold off and the bondholders are paid off from the proceeds. Equipment trust certificates are serial bonds, meaning that part of each payment made to a bondholder is interest and part is repaid principal. In this way the loan amount never exceeds the collateral value.

Income Bonds

Income bonds only pay interest to bondholders if the company that issues them makes money. This is the only type of bond where failure to pay bondholders their scheduled interest in a timely fashion does not lead to immediate default. Usually, income bonds are issued by a company in bankruptcy. When facing bankruptcy, a company will meet with its creditors (usually bondholders) and will agree to issue new income bonds in exchange for the old bonds. To prevent the company landing back in bankruptcy court, the creditors agree that interest will only be paid according to what the company earns.

Ratings Bonds

There are two reliable services that rate bonds, Standard & Poor's and Moody's. These two services rate bonds currently on the market and assign each a letter ranking. Consulting these two ratings is a quick and easy way to determine a particular issue's safety and security. Most, but not all, issues are rated. If a bond is not rated, it could be because the issuer didn't want to pay to have the bond rated, or it could be because the company is too new to have a credit history or credit rating. Just because a bond issue is not rated does not mean that it is an unsafe bond.

Standard & Poor's

Standard & Poor's rates bonds using a letter-grade system. Bonds with letter grades of BBB or higher are referred to as "Investment Grade," and those with ratings lower than BBB are referred to as "Speculative Grade." Standard & Poor's assigns either a plus or a minus sign to indicate a bond's relative strength within its category. For instance, a grade of AAA+ indicates that a bond is at the high end of the AAA category.

Here is the Standard & Poor's rating system:

AAA Bonds of the highest quality

AA   High quality debt obligations

A   Bonds that have a strong capacity to pay interest and principal but may be susceptible to adverse effects

BBB Bonds that have an adequate capacity to pay interest and principal but are more vulnerable to adverse economic conditions or changing circumstances

BB   Bonds of lower-medium grade with few desirable investment characteristics

B   Primarily speculative bonds with great uncertainties and major risk if exposed to adverse conditions

CCC Bonds in poor standing that may be defaulted

C   Income bonds on which no interest is being paid

D   Bonds in default

Moody's

Moody's uses a rating system very similar to Standard & Poor's. Bonds with ratings of Baa or greater are considered "Investment Grade." With a rating of lower than Baa a bond is considered "Speculative Grade." Instead of using plus and minus symbols to indicate a bond's relative strength within a category,

Moody's uses a numbering system:

1	indicates the highest level within a category
2	indicates the middle of a category
3	indicates the low end of a category

For example, a rating of Aaa1 would indicate that this bond occupies the highest level inside the Aaa level.

Here is the Moody's rating system:

Aaa   Bonds of highest quality

Aa   Bonds of high quality

A   Bonds whose security of principal and interest is considered adequate but may be impaired in the future

Baa   Bonds of medium grade that are neither highly protected nor poorly secured

Ba   Bonds of speculative quality whose future cannot be considered well ensured

B   Bonds that lack characteristics of a desirable investment

Caa   Bonds in poor standing that may be defaulted

Ca   Speculative bonds that are often in default

C   Bonds with little probability of any investment value

High-yield or "Junk" Bonds

High-yield or "junk" bonds are different from most other bonds. They do not have some of the advantages of other bonds: they provide no tax benefits, and by their very nature put their own principal at risk. A high-yield bond is a bond issued by a company that is considered to be a higher credit risk; high-yield bonds are considered speculative grade. The chance of default with this type of bond is higher than for other bonds; however, "junk" bond yields are higher than those of bonds of better credit quality.

Industry regulators use the bond-rating system as a way to differentiate between various types of bonds. Historically, most investors have restricted their bond interests to investment grade bonds; speculative grade bonds have tended to carry negative connotations and have not been widely held in investment portfolios in the past. Mainstream investors and investment dealers would not deal in these bonds at all. They became known as "junk" bonds because few people would accept the risk of owning them.

Before the 1980s, most junk bonds existed because of a decline in the credit quality of former investment grade issuers. The resulting bonds were known as "fallen angels." The advent of modern portfolio theory in recent decades has meant that financial researchers began to observe that the "risk-adjusted" returns for portfolios of junk bonds were quite high. The credit risk of these bonds was more than compensated for by their higher yields. Underwriters began intentionally issuing new bonds that were lower than investment grade. This led to some very shady and convoluted disbursements of junk bonds in the late 1980s which ended in financial scandal and the collapse of many lower-rated issuers. However, the variety and number of high-yield issues recovered in the 1990s and the junk bond market is currently thriving. A number of mutual funds invest exclusively in high-yield bonds, which have continued to produce high risk-adjusted returns.

Final Word on Bonds

Bonds are a good way to invest your money if you

are concerned about preserving your erosion and are attracted to the guaranteed long-term income that bonds can provide. However, the worst time to purchase bonds is during a recession, because many people and institutions tend to purchase bonds during economic downturns, which raises bond prices. Coupled with this is the fact that during a recession banks will often lower interest rates in the hopes of stimulating the economy, which is bad news for the bond market because it results in lower returns. Junk bonds can produce high yields, particularly during the recovery period of a recession, but as we have seen, they are not the safest form of investment and are not for all investors.

Other Investments

Mutual Funds

The variety and number of mutual funds on the market today is astonishing. A mutual fund is an investment tool that allows small investors access to a well diversified portfolio of equities, bonds, and other securities. Every mutual fund issues a prospectus, which describes the fund's investment policies, objectives, risks, costs and historical performance data. The prospectus will, in essence, describe the investment style of the fund. The fund's net asset value (NAV) is determined each day. Each mutual-fund portfolio is invested to match the objective stated in the investor agreement or prospectus and each shareholder participates in the gain or loss of the fund.

There are two main advantages to mutual funds:

• **Diversification** Buying a mutual fund gives an

investor instant holdings in several different companies, providing a certain degree of stability to the investment

• **Liquidity** Like individual stocks, a mutual-fund investment can be converted into cash very quickly.

There are also a number of disadvantages to mutual funds:

• **Fund Management** The average mutual fund manager generally doesn't make any better stock picks than anyone else. At the same time, mutual fund companies pay their managers and analysts very well, and these costs will be passed on to you as a mutual fund investor. Most funds charge each of their investors an annual management fee generally ranging from 0.5% to 1% of the fund's asset value.

• **Control** Unlike when you pick your own individual stocks, you have no say in what stocks are put in your portfolio.

• **Dilution** Some mutual funds become so large and encompass so many stocks that the gains made by the fund's best-performing holdings are offset by all its worst-performing stocks.

Types of Mutual Funds

Bond Funds

Bond mutual funds are invested in various kinds of bonds.

General Equity Funds

Stocks represent part ownership, or equity, in corporations, and the goal of stock ownership is to see the value of the companies increase over time. Stocks are often categorized by their capitalization (or market cap), and like many other things come in three basic sizes: small, medium, and large. Many mutual funds invest primarily in companies of one of these sizes and are classified as large-cap, mid-cap, or small-cap funds. Additionally, mutual funds are often categorized by the *type* of stocks they consist of: "growth funds and "value" funds are the two most common classifications.

Balanced Funds

Balanced funds consist of some stocks and some bonds. A typical balanced fund might contain about 50% to 65% stocks and hold the rest of the shareholders' money in bonds and cash. It is important to know the distribution of stocks and bonds in a specific balanced fund to understand the risks and rewards of that fund.

Global and International Funds

Global and international funds invest in companies whose headquarters are outside of North America. In general, international funds are more volatile than domestic funds. International funds generally invest in foreign companies exclusively, while global funds may invest in some North American-based companies in addition to foreign companies.

Sector Funds

Sector funds concentrate their investments in one particular sector of the economy: technology, banking, computers, and so on. Sector funds can be very volatile because the fate of a particular sector can change rapidly and repeatedly within the broader market.

Index Funds

An index fund consists of shareholdings that correspond to those measured by a certain market index such as the Standard & Poor's 500 Composite Stock Price Index. Index funds differ from actively managed mutual funds in that they do not involve any stock picking by fund management; they simply replicate the returns of the specific index.

Exchange Traded Funds

Another option for the world-weary investor comes in the form of exchange traded funds. An exchange traded fund, or ETF, is similar to a mutual fund, but is traded on a stock exchange like a stock. Exchange traded index investments have become especially popular in recent years, and are now available to track many broad indexes, like the S&P 500, the Nasdaq 100, and the Dow Jones Industrial Average, as well as narrowly defined sector and specialty indexes. With these indexed investments the goal of the ETF manager is not to outperform the market, but to match the market's performance as closely as possible. Over long periods of time, brokers and mutual-fund managers hardly ever outperform the markets they invest in. Add to this the fact that they charge you for their advice and management, and you must consider the possibility that your investment might not equal the market's performance. ETFs have much lower fees to pay when compared to mutual funds. Instead of analyzing the market to anticipate how particular stocks will perform in the future, an ETF manager simply matches what is occurring in the market.

Safe Money

At certain times, especially when the economy is heading into a recession, there are not a lot of lucrative investment options available. So what do you do with your cash? Are there any safe harbors in a bearish market?

Certificates of Deposit

A certificate of deposit (CD) is essentially a loan from an individual to a bank. In exchange for the investor promising not to demand repayment of the loan before a certain amount of time has passed, the bank pays a certain rate of interest. Generally, the longer you tie your money up, the higher the interest rate will be. The advantage of CDs is that you know exactly how much interest you will make on your investment, because payments are predetermined. However, your money can be tied up for a relatively long period of time, and interest rate fluctuations may affect the value of your CD.

Money-market Accounts

A money-market account is essentially a mutual fund that attempts to keep its share price at $1. Professional money managers will take your cash and invest it in government treasury bills, savings bonds, certificates of deposit, and other safe and conservative investments. You are paid the interest that these investments earn. The advantage of a money-market account over a CD is that money markets do not require that your capital be tied up over the long term. As soon as you put your money into this kind of account, you are paid a relatively high rate of interest, you have immediate access to your money and you can write checks out of the account. The disadvantage of money-market accounts is that interest rates fluctuate, making it difficult to predict returns over long periods of time. As well, during a recessionary period, interest rates tend to go down as the central bank tries to stimulate consumer and investment spending—this will mean lower returns on your money-market account.

Appendix A: Creditor List

Creditor	Address	Phone #	Account #	Collateral (if any)

Appendix B: Debts Owed

Creditor	Balance owed	Number of payments	Monthly payments	Payment due date	Amount last paid	Date of last payment	Legal action taken	Collection agency

Appendix C: Monthly Living

Week	1	2	3	4
Housing				
Mortgage payment/rent				
Utilities				
Insurance				
Maintenance and repair				
Property taxes				
Food				
Groceries				
Meals eaten out				
Transportation				
Car payment				
Gas				
Insurance				
License/registration fees				
Parking/tolls				
Public transportation				
Insurance				
Car				
Health				
Life/disability				
Clothing				
Purchases				
Cleaning/laundry				
Alteration/repairs				
Health				
Medicine				
Hospital				
Doctor				
Dentist				
Total, this page				

Week	1	2	3	4
Total from last page				
Child care				
Personal				
Tuition/course fees				
Barber/hairdresser				
Toiletries/cosmetics				
Communication				
Telephone				
Internet				
Postage/stationary				
Recreation				
Books/newspapers				
Movies/plays/concerts				
Cable fees				
Alcohol/tobacco				
Vacation				
Sporting goods				
Other				
Donations				
Gifts				
Credit cards				
Card 1				
Card 2				
Card 3				
Card 4				
Loan payments				
Miscellaneous				
Total				

Appendix D: Debt Payment Plan

Creditor	% of total debt	Original payment	Amount to be paid	Jan.	Feb.	Mar.	April	May	June	July	Aug.	Sept.	Oct.	Nov.	Dec.

Appendix E: Bankruptcy Courts

Alabama

Middle District, U.S. Bankruptcy Court, P.O. Box 1248, Montgomery, AL 36102, (334) 206-6300, www.almb.uscourts.gov

Northern District, Bankruptcy Clerk, U.S. Bankruptcy Court, 1800 5th. Ave. N., Birmingham, AL 35203, (205) 731-0850, www.alnb.uscourts.gov

Southern District, Bankruptcy Clerk, U.S. Bankruptcy Court, 201 St. Louis St., Mobile, AL 36602, (334) 441-5391, www.alsb.uscourts.gov

Alaska

U.S. Bankruptcy Court, 605 West 4th Ave., Ste. 138, Anchorage, AK 99501-2296, (907) 271-2655, www.akb.uscourts.gov

Arizona

Bankruptcy Court, 110 S. Church St., Ste. 8112, Tucson, AZ 85701, (520) 620-7500, www.ecf.azb.uscourts.gov

Arkansas

U.S. Bankruptcy Court, 300 W. 2nd., Ste. 111, Little Rock, AR 72201, (501) 918-5506, www.arb.uscourts.gov

California

Central District, U.S. Bankruptcy Court, 255 East Temple St., Los Angeles, CA 90012, (213) 894-6244, www.cacb.uscourts.gov

Eastern District, 2656 U.S. Courthouse, 1130 O St., Fresno, CA 93721, (559) 498-7217, www.caeb.uscourts.gov

Northern District, U.S. Bankruptcy Court, 235 Pine St.,

19th Fl. P.O. Box 7241, San Francisco, CA 94120-7341, (413) 268-2300, www.canb.uscourts.gov
Southern District, U.S. Bankruptcy Court, 325 West F. St., San Diego, CA 92101-6991, (619) 557-6582, www.casb.uscourts.gov

Colorado
U.S. Custom House, 721 19th St., Denver, CO 80202-2508, (303) 844-4045, www.cob.uscourts.gov

Connecticut
U.S. Bankruptcy Court, 157 Church St., 18th Fl., New Haven, CT 06510, (203) 773-2009, www.ctb.uscourts.gov

Delaware
U.S. Bankruptcy Court, 824 Market St., 5th Fl., Wilmington, DE 19801, (302) 252-2900, www.deb.uscourts.gov

Florida
Middle District, U.S. Bankruptcy Court, 801 N. Florida Ave., Tampa, FL 33602, (813) 301-5162, www.flmb.uscourts.gov
Northern District, U.S. Bankruptcy Court, Ste. 3120, 227 North Bronough St., Tallahasee, FL 32301-1378, (904) 942-8933, www.ganb.uscourts.gov
Southern District, U.S. Bankruptcy Court, 51 SW First Ave. Rm. 1517, Miami, FL 33130, (305) 536-5216, www.flsb.uscourts.gov

Georgia
Middle District, Bankruptcy Clerk, P.O. Drawer 1957, 433 Cherry St., Macon, GA, (912) 752-3506, www.gamb.uscourts.gov
Northern District, U.S. Bankruptcy Court, 75 Spring St. SW, Rm. 1431, Atlanta, GA 30303, (404) 215-1000, www.ganb.uscourts.gov
Southern District, Bankruptcy Clerk, P.O. Box 8347,

Savannah, GA 31412, (912) 650-4020

Hawaii

U.S. Bankruptcy Clerk, 1132 Bishop St., Ste. 250L, Honolulu, HI 96813, (808) 522-8100, ext. 116

Idaho

U.S. Bankruptcy Court, 550 West Fort St., Boise, ID 83724, (208) 334-1074, www.id.uscourts.gov

Illinois

Central District, 226 U.S. Courthouse, 600 E. Monroe St., Springfield, IL 62701, (217) 492-4551

Northern District, U.S. Bankruptcy Court, 219 South Dearborn St., Chicago, IL 60604, (312) 435-5694, www.ilnb.uscourts.gov

Southern District, U.S. Bankruptcy Court, 401 S. Missouri, East St. Louis, IL, (219) 236-8247, www.ilsb.uscourts.gov

Indiana

Northern District, U.S. Bankruptcy Court, 401 S. Michigan St, South Bend, IN 46634-7003, (219) 968-2100, www.innb.uscourts.gov

Southern District, 116 U.S Courthouse, 46 East Ohio St., Indianapolis, IN 46204, (317) 229-3800, www.insb. uscourts.gov

Iowa

Northern District, Bankruptcy Clerk, P.O. Box 74890, Cedar Rapids, IA 52407, (319) 286-2200, www.ianb. uscourts.gov

Southern District, Bankruptcy Clerk, U.S. Courthouse Annex, 110 E. Court Ave., Des Moines, IA 50309-2050, (515) 284-6230

Kansas

U.S. Bankruptcy Court, 401 North Market St., Wichita, KS 67202, (316) 269-6486, www.ksb. uscourts.gov

Kentucky

Eastern District, U.S. Bankruptcy Court, P.O. Box 1111, Lexington, KY 40588, (606) 233-2608, www.kyeb. uscourts.gov

Western District, 546 U.S. Courthouse, 601 West Broadway, Louisville, KY 40202, (502) 627-5700, www.kywb.uscourts.gov

Louisiana

Eastern District, U.S. Bankruptcy Court, 601 Hale Boggs Federal Bldg., 501 Magazine St., New Orleans, LA 70130-3386, (504) 589-7878, www.laeb. uscourts.gov

Middle District, U.S. Bankruptcy Court, 707 Florida St., Ste. 119, Baton Rouge, LA 70801, (504) 389-0211

Western District, U.S. Bankruptcy Court, Ste. 2201, Fannin St., Shreveport, LA 71101, (318) 445-1890, www.lawb.uscourts.gov

Maine

U.S. Bankruptcy Court, 537 Congress St., 2nd Fl., Portland, ME, (207) 780-3482, www.meb.uscourts.gov

Maryland

U.S. Bankruptcy Court, 101 West Lombard St., Baltimore, MD 21201, (410) 962-2688, www.mdb. uscourts.gov

Massachusetts

Bankruptcy Clerk, Thomas O'Neil Federal Bldg., U.S. Bankruptcy Court, 10 Causeway St., Boston, MA 02222-1074, (617) 565-6050, www.mab.uscourts.gov

Michigan

Eastern District, U.S. Bankruptcy Court, 211 W. Fort St., 21 st. Fl., Detroit, MI 48226, (313) 234-0068, www.mieb.uscourts.gov

Western District, U.S. Bankruptcy Court, Gerald Ford

Federal Bldg., 110 Michigan St. NW, Grand Rapids, MI 49501, (616) 456-2693, www.miwb.uscourts.gov

Minnesota

301 U.S. Courthouse, 300 South Fourth St., Minneapolis, MN 55415, (612) 664-5200, www.mnb. uscourts.gov

Mississippi

Northern District, Bankruptcy Clerk, P.O. Drawer 867, Aberdeen, MS 39730-0867, (601) 369-2596

Southern District, U.S. Bankruptcy Court, 725 Washington Loop, Rm. 117, Biloxi, MS 39530, (228) 432-5542

Missouri

Eastern District, U.S. Bankruptcy Court, 211 North Broadway, 7th Fl., St. Louis, MO 63102-2734, (314) 425-4222, www.moeb.uscourts.gov

Western District, Bankruptcy Clerk, 1800 U.S. Courthouse, 400 E. 9th St., Kansas City, MO 64106, (816) 512-1800, www.mowb.uscourts.gov

Montana

Bankruptcy Clerk, 273 Federal Bldg., 400 North Main St., Butte, MT 50701, (406) 782-1043, www.mtb. uscourts.gov

Nebraska

Bankruptcy Clerk, P.O. Box 428, Downtown Station, Omaha, NE 68101, (402) 221-4687

Nevada

U.S. Bankruptcy Court, 300 Las Vegas Blvd. S., Las Vegas, NV 89101, (702) 388-6257, www.nvb. uscourts.gov

New Hampshire

U.S. Bankruptcy Court, 275 Chestnut St., Rm. 404, Manchester, NH 03101, (603) 666-7626, www.nhb. uscourts.gov

New Jersey

U.S. Bankruptcy Court, 50 Walnut St., 3rd Fl., Newark, NJ 07102, (973) 645-3930, www.njb. uscourts.gov

New Mexico

Bankruptcy Clerk, P.O. Box 546, Albuquerque, NM 87103, (505) 248-6500, www.nmcourt.fed.us/bkdocs/

New York

Eastern District, U.S. Bankruptcy Court, 75 Clinton St., Brooklyn, NY 11201, (718) 330-2188

Northern District, Senior Court Unit Exec., James T. Foley Courthouse, 445 Broadway Street, Albany, NY 12207, (518) 431-0188, www.nynb.uscourts.gov

Southern District, U.S. Bankruptcy Court, One Bowling Green, 6th Fl., New York, NY 10004-11408, (212) 668-2870, www.nysb.uscourts.gov

Western District, 250 U.S. Courthouse, 300 Perl St., Ste. 250, Buffalo, NY 14202, (716) 551-4130, www.nywb. uscourts.gov

North Carolina

Eastern District, Bankruptcy Clerk, P.O. Drawer 2807, Wilson, NC 27894-2807, (252) 237-0248 x143, (919) 846-4752 (Raleigh), www.nceb.uscourts.gov

Middle District, Bankruptcy Clerk, P.O. Box 26100, Greensboro, NC 27402, (336) 333-5647, www.ncmb. uscourts.gov

Western District, Bankruptcy Clerk, 104 Federal Bldg., 401 West Trade St., Charlotte, NC 28202, (704) 350-7500, www.ncwb.uscourts.gov

North Dakota

U.S. Bankruptcy Court, 655 First Ave. N., Ste. 210, Fargo, ND 58102, (701) 297-7140, www.ndb. uscourts.gov

Ohio

Northern District, U.S. Bankruptcy Court, Key Tower, 31st Fl., 127 Public Square, Cleveland, OH 44114, (216) 522-4373, www.ohnb.uscourts.gov

Southern District, U.S. Bankruptcy Court, 170 North High Street, Columbus, OH 43215, (614) 469-2087

Oklahoma

Eastern District, Bankruptcy Clerk, P.O. Box 1347, Okmulgee, OK 74447, (918) 758-0127

Northern District, U.S. Bankruptcy Court, 224 South Boulder St., Ste. 105, Tulsa, OK 74103, (918) 581-7181

Western District, U.S. Bakruptcy Court, 215 Dean A. McGee Ave., Oklahoma City, OK 73102, (405) 609-5700

Oregon

U.S. Bankruptcy Court, 1001 SW Fifth Ave. #700, Portland, OR 97204, (503) 326-2231, www.orb.uscourts.gov

Pennsylvania

Eastern District, Bankruptcy Clerk, Nix Building, Ste. 400 , 900 Market St., Philadelphia, PA 19107, (215) 408-2800, www.paeb.uscourts.gov

Middle District, Bankruptcy Clerk, 217 Federal Courthouse Bldg., 197 South Main St., Wilkes-Barre, PA 18701, (717) 826-6450

Western District, U.S. Bankruptcy Court, 5414 USX Tower, 600 Grant St., Pittsburgh, PA 15219, (412) 355-3210, www.pawb.uscourts.gov

Rhode Island

U.S. Bankruptcy Court, 380 Westminster Mall, Providence, RI 02903, (401) 528-4477, www.rib.uscourts.gov

South Carolina

Bankruptcy Clerk, P.O. Box 1448, Columbia, SC 29202, (803) 765-5436, www.scb.uscourts.gov

South Dakota

Bankruptcy Clerk, 117 Federal Bldg., 400 South Phillips Ave., Sioux Falls, SD 57117, (605) 330-4541, www.sdb.uscourts.gov

Tennessee

Eastern District, U.S. Bankruptcy Court, 31 E. 11th St., Chattanooga, TN 37402, (865) 545-4279, www.tneb. uscourts.gov

Middle District, U.S. Customs House, 701 Broadway, Nashville, TN 37203, (615) 736-7590, www.tnmb. uscourts.gov

Western District, U.S. Bankruptcy Court, 200 Jefferson Ave., 5th Fl., Memphis, TN 38103, (901) 328-3500, www.tnwb.uscourts.gov

Texas

Eastern District, U.S. Bankruptcy Court, 211 W. Ferguson St., 4th Fl., Tyler, TX 75702, (903) 590-1212, www.txeb.uscourts.gov

Northern District, U.S. Bankruptcy Court, 1100 Commerce St., Suite 12 A24, Dallas, TX 75242, (800) 442-6850, www.txnb.uscourts.gov

Southern District, U.S Bankruptcy Court, 615 Leopard St. Ste. 113, Corpus Christi, (512) 888-3484, www.txsb.uscourts.gov

Western District, U.S. Bankruptcy Court, 903 San Jacinto Blvd. #322, Austin, TX 78701, (512) 916-5238, www.txwb.uscourts.gov

Utah

361 U.S. Courthouse, 350 South Main St., Salt Lake City, UT 84101, (801) 524-6687, www.utc.uscourts.gov

Vermont

U.S. Bankruptcy Court, 67 Merchant's Row, 2nd. Fl.,

Rutland, VT 05702, (802) 776-2000, www.vtb. uscourts.gov

Virginia

Eastern District, U.S. Bankruptcy Court, 1100 E. Main St., Ste. 301, Richmond, VA 23219, (804) 916-2400, www.vaeb.uscourts.gov

Western District, Bankruptcy Clerk, 210 Church Ave., P.O. Box 2390, Roanoke, VA 24010, (540) 857-2391, www.vawb.uscourts.gov

Washington

Eastern District, Bankruptcy Clerk, P.O. Box 2164, Spokane, WA 99210, (509) 353-2404, www.waeb. uscourts.gov

Western District, U.S. Bankruptcy Court, 315 Park Place Bldg., 1200 Sixth Ave., Seattle, WA 98101, (206) 553-2751, www.wawb.uscourts.gov

District of Columbia

4400 U.S. Courthouse Ave., 330 Constitution Ave. NW, Washington, DC 20001, (202) 273-0042

West Virginia

Northern District, Bankruptcy Clerk, P.O. Box 70, Wheeling, WV 26003, (304) 233-1655

Southern District, U.S. Bankruptcy Court, 300 Virginia St. E., Charleston, WV 25301, (304) 347-3000

Wisconsin

Eastern District, 126 U.S. Courthouse, 517 East Wisconsin Ave., Milwaukee, WI 53202, (414) 297-3291

Western District, Bankruptcy Clerk, P.O. Box 548, Madison, WI 53701-0548, (608) 264-5178, www.wiw. uscourts.gov

Wyoming

U.S. Bankruptcy Court, 2120 Capitol Ave., Cheyenne WY 82003, (307) 772-2191, www.wyb.uscourts.gov

Appendix F: State Labor Offices

Alabama

Dept. of Labor, P.O. Box 303500, Montgomery, AL 36130-3500, phone: 334-242-3460, fax: 334-240-3417, internet: www.dir.state.al.us

Alaska

Dept. of Labor, P.O. Box 21149, Juneau, AK 99802-1149, phone: 907-465-2700, fax: 907-465-2784, internet: www.labor.state.ak.us

Arizona

Industrial Commission, P.O. Box 19070, Phoenix, AZ 85005-9070, phone: 602-542-4411, fax: 602-542-3104, internet: www.ica.state.az.us

Arkansas

Dept. of Labor, 10421 West Markham, Little Rock, AR 72205, phone: 501-682-4541, fax: 501-682-4535, internet: www.state.ar.us/labor

California

Dept. of Industrial Relations, 455 Golden Gate Ave., 10th Floor, San Francisco, CA 94102, phone: 415-703-5050, fax: 415-703-5059, internet: www.dir.ca.gov

Colorado

Dept. of Labor and Employment, 2 Park Central, Ste. 400, 1515 Arapahoe St., Denver, CO 80202-2117, phone: 303-620-4701, fax: 303-620-4714

Connecticut

Labor Dept., 200 Folly Brook Blvd., Wethersfield, CT 06109-1114, phone: 860-263-6505, fax: 860-263-6529, internet: www.ctdol.state.ct.us

Delaware

Dept. of Labor, 4425 N. Market St., 4th Floor,

Wilmington, DE 19802, phone: 302-761-8000, fax: 302-761-6621, internet: www.delawareworks.com

District of Columbia

Dept. of Employment Services, Employment Security Bldg., 500 "C" St., NW, Ste. 600, Washington, D.C. 20001, phone: 202-724-7100, fax: 202-724-5683, internet: www.does.ci.washington.dc.us

Florida

Dept. of Labor and Employment Security, 2012 Capitol Circle, S.E., Hartman Bldg., Ste. 303, Tallahassee, FL 32399-2152, phone: 850-922-7021, fax: 904-488-8930, internet: www.state.fl.us/dles/ or www.MyFlorida.com

Georgia

Dept. of Labor, Sussex Place – Room 600, 148 International Blvd., N.E., Atlanta, GA 30303, phone: 404-656-3011, fax: 404-656-2683, internet: www.dol.state.ga.us

Guam

Dept. of Labor, Government of Guam, P.O. Box 9970, Tamuning, GU 96931-9970, phone: 671-475-0101, fax: 671-477-2988

Hawaii

Dept. of Labor and Industrial Relations, 830 Punchbowl St., Room 321, Honolulu, HI 96813, phone: 808-586-8844, fax: 808-586-9099, internet: www.dlir.state.hi.us

Idaho

Dept. of Labor, 317 W. Main St., Boise, ID 83735-0001, phone: 208-334-6110, fax: 208-334-6430, internet: www.labor.state.id.us

Illinois

Dept. of Labor, 160 N. LaSalle St., 13th Floor, Ste. C-1300, Chicago, IL 60601, phone: 312-793-1808, fax:

312-793-5257, internet: www.state.il.us/agency/idol

Indiana

Dept. of Labor, 402 West Washington St., Room W195, Indianapolis, IN 46204-2739, phone: 317-232-2378, fax: 317-233-5381, internet: www.state.in.us/labor or teenworker.org

Iowa

Division of Labor Services, 1000 East Grand Ave., Des Moines, IA 50319, phone: 515-281-3447, fax: 515-281-4698, internet: www.state.ia.us/iwd

Kansas

Dept. of Human Resources, 401 S.W. Topeka Blvd., Topeka, KS 66603, phone: 785-296-7474, fax: 785-368-6294, internet: www.hr.state.ks.us

Kentucky

Kentucky Labor Cabinet, 1047 U.S. Hwy. 127 S., Ste. 4, Frankfort, KY 40601, phone: 502-564-3070, fax: 502-564-5387, internet: www.state.ky.us/agencies/labor/labrhome.htm

Louisiana

Dept. of Labor, P.O. Box 94094, Baton Rouge, LA 70804-9094, phone: 225-342-3011, fax: 225-342-3778, internet: www.ldol.state.la.us

Maine

Dept. of Labor, 20 Union St., P.O. Box 259, Augusta, ME 04332-0259, phone: 207-287-3788, fax: 207-287-5292

Maryland

Dept. of Labor, Licensing and Regulation, 500 N. Calvert St., Ste. 401, Baltimore, MD 21202, phone: 410-230-6020 ext. 1393, fax: 410-333-0853, internet: www.dllr.state.md.us

Massachusetts

Dept. of Labor & Work Force Development, 1

Ashburton Place, Rm. 2112, Boston, MA 02108, phone: 617-727-6573, fax: 617-727-1090, internet: www.detma.org/index.htm or www.state.ma.us

Michigan

Dept. of Consumer & Industry Services, P.O. Box 30004, Lansing, MI 48909, phone: 517-373-3034, fax: 517-373-2129, internet: www.cis.state.mi.us/bsr/divisions/whd/home.htm

Minnesota

Dept. of Labor and Industry, 443 Lafayette Rd., St. Paul, MN 55155, phone: 651-296-2342, fax: 651-282-5405, internet: www.doli.state.mn.us

Mississippi

Employment Security Commission, P.O. Box 1699, Jackson, MS 39215-1699, phone: 601-961-7400, fax: 601-961-7406, internet: www.mesc.state.ms.us

Missouri

Dept. of Labor & Industrial Relations, P.O. Box 504, Jefferson City, MO 65102, phone: 573-751-9691, fax: 573-751-4135, internet: www.solir.state.mo.us

Montana

Dept. of Labor and Industry, P.O. Box 1728, Helena, MT 59624-1728, phone: 406-444-9091, fax: 406-444-1394, internet: www.dli.state.mt.us

Nebraska

Dept. of Labor, 550 South 16th St., Box 94600, Lincoln, NE 68509-4600, phone: 402-471-9792, fax: 402-471-2318, internet: www.dol.state.ne.us

Nevada

Business and Industry, 555 E. Washington Ave., Ste. 4100, Las Vegas, NV 89101, phone: 702-486-2650, fax: 702-486-2660, internet: www.state.nv.us/labor

New Hampshire

Dept. of Labor, 95 Pleasant St., Concord, NH 03301,

phone: 603-271-3171, fax: 603-271-6852, internet: www.state.nh.us/dol

New Jersey

Dept. of Labor, John Fitch Plaza, 13th Fl., Ste. D, P.O. Box CN 110, Trenton, NJ 08625-0110, phone: 609-292-2323, fax: 609-633-9271, internet: www.state.nj.us/labor

New Mexico

Dept. of Labor, P.O. Box 1928, 401 Broadway, N.E., Albuquerque, NM 87103-1928, phone: 505-841-8408, fax: 505-841-8491, internet: www3.state.nm.us/dol

New York

Dept. of Labor, State Campus, Bldg. 12, Albany, NY 12240, phone: 518-457-2741, fax: 518-457-6908 or 345 Hudson St., New York, NY 10014-0675, phone: 212-352-6000, internet: www.labor.state.ny.us

North Carolina

Dept. of Labor, 4 W. Edenton St., Raleigh, NC 27601-1092, phone: 919-733-0360, fax: 919-733-6197, internet: www.dol.state.nc.us

North Dakota

Dept. of Labor, State Capitol Bldg., 600 East Blvd., Dept. 406, Bismark, ND 58505-0340, phone: 701-328-2660, fax: 701-328-2031, internet: www.state.nd.us/labor

Ohio

Division of Labor and Worker Safety, 50 West B Rd. St., 28th floor, Columbus, OH 43216, phone: 614-644-2239, fax: 614-728-8639-5650, internet: www.state.oh.us/ohio/agency.htm

Oklahoma

Dept. of Labor, 4001 N. Lincoln Blvd., Oklahoma City, OK 73105-5212, phone: 405-528-1500, ext. 200, fax: 405-528-5751, internet: www.state.ok.us/~okdol

Oregon

Bureau of Labor and Industries, 800 NE Oregon St. #32, Portland, OR 97232, phone: 503-731-4070, fax: 503-731-4103, internet: www.boli.state.or.us

Pennsylvania

Dept. of Labor and Industry, 1700 Labor and Industry Bldg., 7th and Forster Sts., Harrisburg, PA 17120, phone: 717-787-3756, fax: 717-787-8826, internet: www.li.state.pa.us

Puerto Rico

Dept. of Labor & Human Resources, Edificio Prudencio Rivera Martinez, 505 Munoz Rivera Ave., G.P.O. Box 3088, Hato Rey, PR 00918, phone: 787-754-2119 or 2120, fax: 787-753-9550

Rhode Island

Dept. of Labor and Training, 1511 Pontiac Ave., Cranston, RI 02920, phone: 401-462-8870, fax: 401-462-8872, internet: www.det.state.ri.us

South Carolina

Dept. of Labor, Licensing & Regulations, Synergy Center – King St. Bldg., 110 Center View Dr., P.O.Box 11329, Columbia, SC 29211-1329, phone: 803-896-4300, fax: 803-896-4393, internet: www.llr.state.sc.us

South Dakota

Dept. of Labor, 700 Governors Dr., Pierre, SD 57501-2291, phone: 605-773-3101, fax: 605-773-4211, internet: www.state.sd.us/dol/dol.htm

Tennessee

Dept. of Labor, Andrew Johnson Tower, 710 James Robertson Pky., 8th Floor, Nashville, TN 37243-0655, phone: 615-741-6642, fax: 615-741-5078, internet: www.state.tn.us

Texas

Texas Workforce Commission, 101 East 15th St., Rm. 618, Austin, TX 78778, phone: 512-463-0735, fax: 512-475-2321, internet: www.twc.state.tx.us

Utah

Utah Labor Commission, P.O. Box 146600, Salt Lake City, UT 84111-2316, phone: 801-530-6880, fax: 801-530-6390, internet: www.labor.state.ut.us

Vermont

Dept. of Labor & Industry, National Life Bldg., Drawer #20, Montpelier, VT 05620-3401, phone: 802-828-2288, fax: 802-828-0408, internet: www.state.vt.us/labind

Virgin Islands

Dept. of Labor, 2303 Church St., Christiansted, St. Croix, U.S. VI 00820-4612 , phone: 340-773-1994, ext. 230, fax: 340-773-0094, internet: www.vidol.org

Virginia

Dept. of Labor and Industry, Powers-Taylor Bldg., 13 S. 13th, Richmond, VA 23219, phone: 804-786-2377, fax: 804-371-6524, internet: www.dli.state.va.us

Washington

Dept. of Labor & Industries, P.O. Box 44001, Olympia, WA 98504-4001, phone: 360-902-4213, fax: 360-902-4202, internet: www.wa.gov/lni

West Virginia

Division of Labor, Bureau of Commerce, State Capitol Complex, Bldg. #3, Room 319, Charleston, WV 25305, phone: 304-558-7890, fax: 304-558-3797, internet: www.state.wv.us/labor

Wisconsin

Dept. of Workforce Development, 201 East Washington Ave., #400, P.O. Box 7946, Madison, WI 53707-7946, phone: 608-266-7552, fax: 608-266-1784, internet: www.dwd.state.wi.us

Wyoming

Labor Standards, Dept. of Employment, U.S. West Bldg., Room 259C, 6101 Yellowstone Rd., Cheyenne, WY 82002, phone: 307-777-7261, fax: 307-777-5633, internet: www.wydoe.state.wy.us/labstd

Glossary

Bank Run: Unexpected (usually large) cash withdrawls from one or more banks brought about by loss of depositer confidence and fear that the bank will close. Bank runs can be contagious and usually result in the authorities stepping in with deposit guarantees.

Book-entry: One form in which Treasury and certain government agency securities are held. Book-entry form consists of an entry on the records of the U.S. Treasury Department, a Federal Reserve Bank, or a financial institution.

Bonus Bill (GI Bill): A bill passed in 1924 that awarded special benefits to war veterans.

Buydown: A lump sum payment made to the creditor by the borrower or by a third party to reduce the amount of some or all of the consumer's periodic payments to repay the indebtedness.

Capital market: The market in which corporate equity and longer-term debt securities (those maturing in more than one year) are issued and traded.

Central bank: Principal monetary authority of a nation, which performs several key functions, including issuing currency and regulating the supply of money and credit in the economy. The Federal Reserve is the central bank of the United States.

Central bank intervention: In order to influence market conditions or exchange rate movements, central banks buy or sell their currency or the currency of other countries.

Certificate of deposit (CD): A form of time deposit at a bank or savings institution; a time deposit cannot be withdrawn before a specified maturity date without being subject to an interest penalty for early withdrawal. Small-denomination CDs are often purchased by individuals. Large CDs of $100,000 or more are often in negotiable form, meaning they can be sold or transferred among holders before maturity.

Consumer Price Index (CPI): A measure of the average amount (price) paid for a market basket of goods and services by a typical U.S. consumer in comparison to the average paid for the same basket in an earlier base year.

Currency appreciation: An increase in the value of one currency relative to another currency. Appreciation occurs when, because of a change in exchange rates, a unit of one currency buys more units of another currency.

Currency depreciation: A decline in the value of one currency relative to another currency. Depreciation occurs when, because of a change in exchange rates, a unit of one currency buys fewer units of another currency.

Currency devaluation: A deliberate downward adjustment in the official exchange rate established, or pegged, by a government against a specified standard, such as another currency or gold.

Currency revaluation: A deliberate upward adjustment in the official exchange rate established, or pegged, by a government against a specified standard, such as another currency or gold.

Cyclical unemployment: Temporary layoff of workers due to downturns in the pace of economic activity.

Demand deposit: A deposit payable on demand, or a time deposit with a maturity period or required notice period of less than 14 days, on which the depository institution does not reserve the right to require at least 14 days written notice of intended withdrawal. Commonly takes the form of a checking account.

Depository institution: Financial institution that obtains its funds mainly through deposits from the public; includes commercial banks, savings and loan associations, savings banks, and credit unions.

Debt to equity ratio: Long-term debt divided by shareholders' equity, showing relationship between long-term funds provided by creditors and funds provided by shareholders; high ratio may indicate high risk, low ratio may indicate low risk.

Discount rate: Interest rate at which an eligible depository institution may borrow funds, typically for a short period, directly from a Federal Reserve Bank. The law requires that the board of directors of each Reserve Bank establish the discount rate every fourteen days subject to the approval of the Board of Governors.

Dividend: Distribution of earnings to shareholders, prorated by the class of security and paid in the form of money, stock, scrip, or, rarely, company products or property. The amount is decided by the Board of Directors and is usually paid quarterly. Mutual fund dividends are paid out of income, usually on a quarterly basis from the fund's investments.

Excess reserves: Amount of reserves held by an institution in excess of its reserve requirement and required clearing balance.

Exchange rate: The price of a country's currency in terms of another country's currency.

Equilibrium real interest rate: The level of the real interest rate that is consistent with the level of long-run output and full employment.

Federal funds rate: The interest rate at which banks borrow surplus reserves and other immediately available funds. The federal funds rate is the shortest short-term interest rate, with maturities on federal funds concentrated in overnight or one-day transactions.

Federal Reserve Bank: The US central bank, comprised of 12 regional Federal Reserve Banks. The Fed manages the money supply through interest rate manipulation and open market activities (buying/selling money, usually in form of Treasury Bills). The Fed also intervenes in the foreign exchange markets if necessary, regulates the banking sector and acts as the federal government's banker.

Federal Reserve System: The central bank of the United States created by Congress, consisting of a seven-member Board of Governors in Washington, D.C., 12 regional Reserve Banks, and depository institutions that are subject to reserve requirements. All national banks are members and state chartered banks may elect to become members. State member banks are supervised by the Board of Governors and the Reserve Banks. Reserve requirements established by the Federal Reserve Board apply to nonmember depository institutions as well as member banks. Both classes of institutions have access to Federal Reserve discount borrowing privileges and Federal Reserve services on an equal basis.

Fiscal policy: Federal government policy regarding taxation and spending, set by Congress and the Administration.

Foreign currency operations: Purchase or sale of the

currencies of other nations by a central bank for the purpose of influencing foreign exchange rates or maintaining orderly foreign exchange markets. Also called foreign-exchange market intervention.

Foreign exchange rate: Price of the currency of one nation in terms of the currency of another nation.

Free Trade Area: A treaty agreement between two or more countries to eliminate tariffs and other barriers to physical (merchandise) trade. Note that each country may set its own tariff rates or non-tariff barriers against other, non-members.

Futures: Contracts that require delivery of a commodity of specified quality and quantity, at a specified price, on a specified future date. Commodity futures are traded on a commodity exchange and are used for both speculation and hedging.

Garnish: to take money owed directly from paychecks.

Gold Standard: the use of gold as the standard value for the money of a country.

Government securities: Securities issued by the U.S. Treasury or federal agencies.

Gross Domestic Product (GDP): The total value of all goods and services produced (or consumed) within a country. On the demand side, GDP comprises private consumption expenditure + government consumption expenditure + gross fixed capital formation + the change in inventories + exports of goods and services - imports of goods and services. On the supply side, GDP includes agriculture, manufacturing, construction, financial services and other producing sectors of the economy. In both cases, what is measured is not transactions but the value added during the exchange of goods or services. One common measure of individual wealth is GDP per capita, which is total GDP divided by the population.

Gross National Product (GNP): GDP, plus income generated by the country's companies and individuals overseas. In most cases, GNP differs from GDP by such a small amount that the terms are used interchangeably. However, where a large share of companies or individuals work overseas (e.g., British Virgin Islands for companies and the Philippines for individuals), the difference can be quite significant.

Hyperinflations: Rapid, out-of-control inflations, at double digit rates per month and more, usually occurring only during wars and periods of severe political instability.

Inflation: A rate of increase in the general price level of all goods and services. (This should not be confused with increases in the prices of specific goods relative to the prices of other goods.)

Inflationary expectations: The rate of increase in the general price level anticipated by the public in the period ahead.

International Monetary Fund (IMF): An international organization with 146 members, including the United States. The main functions of the International Monetary Fund are to lend funds to member nations to finance temporary balance of payments problems, to facilitate the expansion and balanced growth of international trade, and to promote international monetary cooperation among nations. The IMF also creates special drawing rights (SDRs), which provide member nations with a source of additional reserves. Member nations are required to subscribe to a Fund quota, paid mainly in their own currency. The IMF grew out of the Bretton Woods Conference of 1944.

Lender of last resort: As the nation's central bank, the Federal Reserve has the authority and financial resources to act as "lender of last resort" by extending credit to depository institutions or to other entities in unusual circumstances involving a national or regional emergency where failure to obtain credit would have a severe adverse impact on the economy.

Load Fund: Mutual fund that is sold for a sales charge by a brokerage firm or other sales representative. Such funds may be stock, bond or commodity funds, with conservative or aggressive objectives.

Long-term interest rates: Interest rates on loan contracts—or debt instruments such as Treasury bonds or utility, industrial or municipal bonds—having maturities greater than one year. Often called capital market rates.

Margin account: A brokerage account that permits an investor to purchase securities on credit and to borrow on securities already in the account. Buying on credit and borrowing are subject to standards established by the Federal Reserve and by the firm carrying the account. Interest is charged on any borrowed funds only for the period of time the loan is outstanding.

Market interest rates: Rates of interest paid on deposits and other investments, determined by the interaction of the supply of and demand for funds in financial markets.

Monetary policy: A central bank's actions to influence short-term interest rates and the supply of money and credit, as a means of helping to promote national economic goals. Tools of U.S. monetary policy include open market operations, discount rate policy, and reserve requirements.

money stock

• **Ml** – The sum of currency held by the public, plus travelers' checks, plus demand deposits, plus other checkable deposits (i.e., negotiable order of withdrawal [NOW] accounts, and automatic transfer service [ATS] accounts, and credit union share drafts.)

• **M2** – Ml plus savings accounts and small denomination time deposits, plus shares in money market mutual funds (other than those restricted to institutional investors), plus overnight Eurodollars and repurchase agreements

• **M3** – M2 plus large-denomination time deposits at all depository institutions, large denomination term repurchase agreements, and shares in money market mutual funds restricted to institutional investors.

Mutual Fund: Fund operated by an investment company that raises money from shareholders and invests it in stocks, bonds, options, commodities or money market securities.

Natural rate of unemployment: The rate of unemployment that can be sustained in the long run and that is consistent with constant inflation.

New Deal: Programs initiated in the U.S. in the 1930s that were characterized by significantly increased government aid to various economic groups and equally significant increases in government involvement in the economy.

No Load Fund: Mutual Fund offered by an open end investment company that imposes no sales charge (load) on its shareholders. Investors buy shares in no-load funds directly from the fund companies, rather than through a broker as is done in load funds. Many no-load fund families allow switching of assets between stock, bond, and money market funds. The listing of the price of a no-load fund in the newspaper is accompanied by the designation NL. The net asset value, market price and offer prices of this type of fund are exactly the same, since there is no sales charge.

Nominal interest rates: Stated rates of interest paid or earned; often thought of as consisting of a real rate of interest and a premium to compensate for expected inflation.

P/B Ratio (Price/Book Ratio): A stock analysis statistic in which the price of a stock is divided by the reported book value (as of the date specified) of the issuing firm.

P/C Ratio (Price/Cash Flow Ratio): A financial ratio that compares stock price with cash flow from operations per outstanding shares.

P/E Ratio (Price/Earnings Ratio): A stock analysis statistic in which the current price of a stock (today's last sale price) is divided by the reported actual (or sometimes projected, which would be forecast) earnings per share of the issuing firm; it is also called the "multiple".

P/S Ratio (Price/Sales Ratio): A financial ratio that compares stock price with sales per share (or market value with total revenue).

Peak: The transition of a business cycle from an expansion to a contraction. The end of an expansion carries the descriptive term peak. At the peak, the economy has reached the highest level of production in recent times. The bad thing about a peak is that it is a turning point, a turning point to a contraction. So even though a peak is the "highest" it is not necessarily something we want. We would prefer never to reach the peak.

Productivity: The amount of physical output for each unit of productive input.

Prorated: To divide, distribute, or assess proportionately.

Purchasing power parity rate (PPP): The exchange rate between any two currencies adjusts to reflect changes in the price levels within the two countries.

Quotas: limits on the amount of foreign goods that can be imported

Real GDP: GDP adjusted for inflation. Real GDP provides the value of GDP in constant dollars, which is used as an indicator of the volume of the nation's final output.

Real interest rates: Interest rates adjusted for the expected erosion of purchasing power resulting from inflation. Technically defined as nominal interest rates minus the expected rate of inflation.

Short Selling: Short selling is the selling of a security that the seller does not own, or any sale that is completed by the delivery of a security borrowed by the seller. Short selling is a legitimate trading strategy. Short sellers assume the risk that they will be able to buy the stock at a more favorable price than the price at which they sold short.

Short-term interest rates: Interest rates on loan contracts—or debt instruments such as Treasury bills, bank certificates of deposit, or commercial paper—

having maturities less than one year. Often called money market rates.

Stagflation: An economic condition characterized by simultaneous inflation, slow growth and high unemployment.

Supply-side economics: Places supply ahead of demand in economic hierarchy. Tax cuts could generate spending and productivity, which would lower unemployment and maintain a suitable rate of inflation, without having to increase the money supply.

Treasury bill: Short-term U.S. Treasury security issued in minimum denominations of $10,000 and usually having original maturities of 3, 6, or 12 months. Investors purchase bills at prices lower than the face value of the bills; the return to the investors is the difference between the price paid for the bills and the amount received when the bills are sold or when they mature. Treasury bills are the type of security used most frequently in open market operations.

Treasury bond: Long-term U.S. Treasury security usually having initial maturities of more than 10 years and issued in denominations of $1,000 or more, depending on the specific issue. Bonds pay interest semi-annually, with principal payable at maturity.

Treasury note: Intermediate-term coupon-bearing U.S. Treasury security having initial maturities from 1 to 10 years and issued in denominations of $1,000 or more, depending on the maturity of the issue. Notes pay interest semi-annually, and the principal is payable at maturity.

Trough: The transition of a business cycle from a contraction to an expansion. The end of a contraction carries the descriptive term trough. At the trough, the economy has reached the lowest level of production in recent times. The good thing about a trough is that it is a turning point, a turning point to an expansion. So even though a trough is the "lowest" it is not necessarily something that's undesirable.

Underwriter: The investment banking firm that brings a company public.

Index